THE DOG
WHISPERER

THE DOG
WHISPERER

HOW TO TRAIN YOUR DOG USING
ITS OWN LANGUAGE

Illustrations by Graeme Sims

GRAEME SIMS

headline

First published in 2008 by
HEADLINE PUBLISHING GROUP

2

Cataloguing in Publication Data is available from the British Library

ISBN 978 0 7553 1698 4

Typeset in Baskerville by Avon DataSet Ltd, Bidford on Avon, Warwickshire

Printed and bound in the UK by
CPI Mackays, Chatham ME5 8TD

Headline's policy is to use papers that are natural, renewable and recyclable
products and made from wood grown in sustainable forests. The logging and
manufacturing processes are expected to conform to the environmental
regulations of the country of origin.

HEADLINE PUBLISHING GROUP
An Hachette Livre UK Company
338 Euston Road
London NW1 3BH

www.headline.co.uk
www.hachettelivre.co.uk

www.graemesims.com

I dedicate this book to you the reader
and more especially to your dogs.
May what is written here bring you even closer together.

Contents

CONTENTS

Acknowledgements

I would like to thank the following for their support, patience and advice:

Darley Anderson, Val Hudson, Lorraine Jerram, Zoe King and Philippa Hobbs.

And, in particular, my wife Maureen for consistently being her.

Plus, of course, my fifteen dogs for allowing me into their world.

A Note from the Author

I wanted this book to be me, warts and all. The words I have chosen are mine and written as I would speak them. They are as they are – including the repeats – in order that the book should serve its intended purpose: *to teach people to train their dogs well.*

Preface

Eleven years ago I started work for the Milky Way theme park in England's West Country. Its purpose was to show country skills to town dwellers. My job was to demonstrate the working intelligence of sheepdogs.

The management was much more enlightened than many theme parks I had heard about. The managing director, Trevor Stanbury, had seen countless demonstrations involving sheep being herded by dogs and reckoned that they all looked the same. I should work just dogs. It would be a unique display rather than one of many.

He reasoned that if I could control more dogs than anybody else had managed, the dog-owning public would find it attractive and much more relevant.

I practised hard throughout the winter with six dogs, using my dog-whispering method. It was a nervous time as I could not be sure that it would work. It was difficult too because sheep provide sheepdogs with focus and motivation, so working them without could have been a real problem.

I decided to make it clearer for the dogs by using a different language for each. Bob would work to commands in German, Annie in Welsh, Molly a Devon dialect, Susie Irish, Wing English, and Ben in Anglo-Saxon.

Each would have different body-language signs and, to complicate it even further, each would have different whistles for distance working.

Working six dogs at the same time with different whistles, different languages and different body-language signs, in front of several thousand people, is like playing three-dimensional chess.

If I didn't manage to achieve my objectives I would fairly quickly be without job and house. Theme parks cannot afford to put on demonstrations that are less than excellent.

A demonstration is much harder than a competition because an entertaining commentary is needed to explain the action.

As the season came closer the publicity started and my picture (with some very flattering copy) appeared just about everywhere. The pressure increased.

Then the day of reckoning came. There was a big crowd sitting on the grassy banks of the natural arena and all of the staff and management had come out to see if the much-vaunted 'new boy' could actually deliver.

Well, he did! It was better than I could have hoped. When I came off the field Trevor was all smiles. 'It was great, absolutely great,' he said. The trouble was, it had lasted just twelve minutes out of the scheduled forty-five. But apparently those twelve minutes had convinced everyone.

For the first five years we delivered four shows a day on six days a week; I was also running a huge dog breeding and training centre. New dogs were added, new techniques learned, and I managed to fill the forty-five-minute slot every time.

For the next six years I earned my living doing shows all over the country.

I was doing one at a seaside resort. The venue was a huge and beautiful park blessed with hard paths that suited joggers, cyclists and dog-walkers. In my whole life I have never seen so many people walking their dogs. They started at dawn and paraded in front of my interested gaze until the end of the long summer weekend.

As I had a lot of waiting between demonstrations I watched them from the vantage point of my caravan. I noticed that very few had any understanding. To be fair, the good ones were pretty competent but they were vastly outnumbered by those who had no idea at all.

Dogs know when other dogs are around, even if they are hidden by caravan walls.

Given that both my Jeep and my caravan prominently display what I do, including a line that says clearly and boldly, 'Shsssh – Dogs Sleeping', it should have been clear that a number of dogs were present.

Dogs are territorial but that did not stop owners from allowing theirs to walk right up to the caravan entrance and linger there as the mood took them.

My dogs saw the need to drive off invaders of their territory so their days were spent in a state of some tension.

Maybe one dog in twenty responded to its owner's 'come here' commands, but even these 'stars' needed the command repeated five or six times.

One woman bribed her dog with a biscuit to leave. She had obviously given up on it responding to any other request. (It took no notice!)

I don't know how many dogs and owners I saw over the three days that I was there but as they came along every two minutes or so there must have been a thousand. There were all sorts of breeds, all in good condition. Their owners certainly scored in the kindness stakes but the ability to actually control their dogs was, in the main, missing.

Very few showed much understanding of how to communicate with their dogs and the commands used were largely ineffective.

The owners I saw knew what to say in a command sense and were aware that their dog would thrive on physical exercise, but they reminded me of someone who tries to unlock a padlock by sawing through the chain rather than using the key designed for the purpose.

This book is that key. It will make a huge difference to your dog-training skills by increasing your understanding of your best friend.

I tell you this by way of a promise. One of the biggest fears about any training method is that it means investing time towards a result that won't be known until completion.

Will it work?

If you follow this method of training faithfully the results will be beyond your greatest expectations.

Don't 'cherry pick': don't give more weight to the bits you like and skip the bits you are not too keen on. When you reach what may appear to be a throwaway line, or an overly simple statement, read it again.

In this book the 'simple' is profound. Each step is like a staircase. If you attempt to jump a step, the top will never be reached and even the very simple will understand that there is only one place to start . . .

This book does not present an alchemy owned only by me. It is a method road-tested many times. It is shareable and you can do it too.

If you walked along our valley road and looked up to the hills you would see a man working fifteen dogs precisely, to the inch. Then you might say, 'I can do that because I only have to manage it with one!'

Introduction

Orphan Annie

S ome things are meant to be. Some event, thought to be small at the time, can change not only the direction of a life but also the thinking that directs it.

I found my first sheepdog in the middle of a busy road. But, hey, I dash ahead of myself . . .

In the space of just a week my wife and I crashed from being well off to being very poor indeed. Our seemingly thriving business collapsed catastrophically through no fault of ours. There was little prospect of being able to pick up the pieces and start over again. The future looked bleak to say the least.

'Poor' is both an everyday grinding reality and a state of mind.

I was fifty, unemployable, without value, *sans* friends, *sans* everything.

The journey from prosperity to poverty is like losing altitude in an uncontrollable way: collision with the ground is a certainty. All the victim can do is hope that it doesn't come too soon and that it isn't too messy when it does.

Going down is rapid and at the time feels irrevocable.

Because of our predicament, we had made the decision to move to rural Devon, thinking that at least the scenery would be beautiful and, most important, this part would be free. So, time, metaphorically speaking, for one last drink (or many) at our old village pub.

Time for some sorrows to be drowned.

As I came out of my front door, I saw a black-and-white dog lying on the white line in the centre of the road. In the same glance I also saw a truck. The cab lights were on so I could see the drama being acted out in the truck. The driver was standing on his brakes in a desperate attempt to avoid running over the dog. He had a German Shepherd sitting next to him, who also seemed to be applying the brakes.

I could hear a fast-moving car approaching on the other side of the road.

In times of great danger, the mind and the eye see things in slow motion. It was as if I had all the time in the world to make a choice.

I could run out into the road, grab the dog (if it did not run away), bring it back to my side of the road and get us both killed by the truck.

I could make a straight-line dash and risk being squashed by the car on the other side.

I could call the dog.

What do you call a dog you do not know, especially when vital seconds are ticking away?

The name 'Annie' came to mind. Orphan Annie.

She responded, rising from the road surface far too slowly, and walked towards me.

It was just fast enough. The rush of air from the truck lifted the fine hairs on her tail. I had her, safe and sound.

I took her indoors to show her to my wife. 'Look what I've found.'

'We shall call her Annie,' she said.

I asked her if I had mentioned that the name I had chosen was the same. No, I hadn't. We had both separately arrived at the same choice and that in itself was bizarre.

Annie was a strange-looking dog. Her body was thin and her ears were enormous and stuck straight up in the air. She smelled like a pigsty.

The next morning, on the way to see the vet, she was sick and chose the car heater as the most suitable receptacle. The car reminded me pungently of that day for several winters.

She was about nine months old; I could speculate for ever (and have) about how she had managed to get to the same place as me at the same moment. She needed me and I needed her, and something or someone had arranged our coming together.

Often, as I look back, I weigh up the odds against what happened that evening and what would happen as a result of our meeting.

She certainly changed my life and my priorities.

Of course we checked as well as we could to make sure she was not just a dog that had got lost. After three months or so we knew that she was ours and that no previous owner was going to pop up and claim her. If they had turned up, I would have had some fairly strong words for them because it most certainly was not a surplus of kindness that had made her leave them.

Over the next year I trained Annie, figuring that her confidence would perhaps return with her growing proficiency. I did it by instinct. I had no idea really how it should be done.

She was intelligent beyond belief and took to the training like a duck to a very attractive millpond.

By the time we moved to Devon she could perform precise, complex manoeuvres as though it was her vocation – which, of course, it was. I was pleased because I had not read a manual or been on a handler's course. I had simply got it right.

About two weeks after our arrival at our new home, the neighbouring farmer's sheep escaped on to the main road. I saw them go by like an uncontrollable woolly juggernaut, heading for town. Then the farmer was banging on my door, asking for help.

As far as we knew, Annie had never seen a sheep before, let alone several hundred, but something amazing happened. I found that the exercises we had practised were absolutely perfect for what we now had to do.

In just a few moves the sheep were back in the safety of their field and Annie and I had not only made a firm friend but had launched ourselves on a new career.

So, I had found a dog, not any old dog but a sheepdog, on a main road just twenty-five miles from London. We had moved to a remote country area where there are far more sheep than people and where skilful sheepdogs and shepherds are treated like royalty.

Suddenly I was in demand, the unemployable very much employed. It was as though we were much-respected natives of the place, rather than incomers. In just one short year I had moved from the hot-house, creative atmosphere of an advertising agency, with its noise, bustle and excitement, to the world of a humble shepherd alone with his dogs and sheep in the hushed, quiet, green places inhabited only by wildlife.

My income was about as much as the advertising agency would have given as a lunch allowance and other people told me what to do, rather than the other way round, but I had found real contentment and self-respect.

As our workload increased, more sheepdogs were added to the team, and before long we could bring sheep back from difficult, inaccessible places quicker than several men, quad bikes and four-wheel drives could manage.

Then I was offered a job as a demonstrator at a theme park and headhunted for a starring role at another. Our skills were honed even more finely.

I began to get into the mind of the dog and speak the same language. Before long my reputation as a trainer spread, and people came from far and wide with problem dogs to ask for my help. Some of the dogs were overly aggressive, others too timid, and one, a sheepdog, was actually afraid of sheep. Most of the problems talked about in this book were dealt with during this period.

The frightened sheepdog turned out to be scared only when he was too close to sheep so, after a lot of thought, I taught him to work at a greater distance away from them, reckoning that the sheep would be more worried about the threat than the actuality, providing the threat was delivered dramatically. In the end I taught him to move decisively so that the sheep would be fooled into thinking he was full of confidence. In other words, I provided him with very good camouflage to hide his fear.

So far I have spent twenty enjoyable years working with dogs in front of large audiences where every single movement is carefully thought out and just has to be successful. But perhaps more important are the hours spent in wild places with only my dogs for company.

I have never met a dog that does not have a large measure of good inside it.

I have never met a dog that could not be trained once the right approach is found.

Most satisfying is the knowledge that there is no such thing as an unlovable dog. Nor was a dog ever born that failed to love the owner who loved it.

If only I could make the same observation about owners.

With dogs it is simple: love them, show that you love them, then use this foundation to build the training on.

I wonder what Annie's previous owner would have thought if he had seen her performing so expertly at a big show as if she was born to the role. Would he have kicked himself? I do hope so!

Annie lived, and worked, for thirteen years. On her last day I picked her up from the vet and carefully carried her body home.

We buried her on a ridge overlooking the farm so that she could see us working.

I was upset, but 'someone' had given her to me and now had taken her away. I was grateful to have had her by me for so long.

Chapter One

The Dog in the
Iron Mask

In all my years as a dog trainer and breeder I had not seen an unhappier dog. He was very different from the carefree, confident puppy we had sold four months earlier. He cringed, his head was down. If tears were a dog's way of showing unhappiness he would have wept torrents of them. My heart went out to him and I felt his pain. I wanted to undo the results of treatment that carried no understanding.

'Don't put your face near him or he'll take it off,'
the owner told me.

The dog in the iron mask: muzzle firmly strapped on, frightened eyes and obviously depressed. Locked in the back of a car like some kind of criminal. No right of appeal, no 'we'll hear your side of the story', just unfathomable punishment.

The owner continued to give advice that contradicted all the observable facts – plus, of course, the expression on the imprisoned dog's face. We agreed to take Bendi back.

I got rid of his human as fast as I could. I was glad to see him drive away. His parting remark was that he hoped to see Bendi in one of my shows – as if the damage he had inflicted could be instantly undone by waving a magic wand.

My wife and I were suddenly alone with 'mad' Bendi. I put him into the back of my Jeep and drove to a quiet field.

I threw his choke chain over a hedge, followed by the offending muzzle. I wanted to demonstrate to him that life was going to change for the better from this point on.

He was free!

The Freedom Test

I watched him closely and he watched me, not knowing what to make of this strange human. Then he ran away as fast as he could. I did not run after him but sat quietly on the grass, not even looking in his direction. About a quarter of an hour went by before I felt him near me. He sniffed the back of my coat. I made sniffing noises, then started to talk, very softly. Eventually he worked his way round to the front of me and looked at my face.

I did what his previous owner had recommended I should not do and made eye contact. Then I touched him gently, and talked to him continually in a soft, soothing voice. He was so het up that I don't think he remembered me – or, if he did, he didn't trust his memory.

After about an hour of doing what he wanted to do I opened the car door on the front passenger side and patted the seat.

It took five minutes of hesitation before he jumped in. I did not reach across him to shut the door (why take a risk?) but got out, walked round the car and shut the door before driving home. He walked straight in through the front door, no doubt remembering it as the gateway to a peaceful place rather than me as the provider of it.

I detected that he was much more relaxed. We put him in the kitchen with a calm and friendly older dog called Jack, and my wife Maureen fed them both an exceptionally tasty dinner.

He slept all evening and at night continued his sleep by my side of the bed, remembering me now and, perhaps, that I was fit to be trusted. He was content and at ease.

I have noticed a huge difference between happy puppies that have been brought back for a social visit to the breeder by their new owner and those that have suffered some kind of trauma. The disturbed puppies recognise the place first and the voice, or smell, of the breeder second. The happy puppies recognise the voice immediately.

Even now, if one of us raises a threatening-looking hand Bendi still flinches, but two years after his return he is a very happy and well-behaved dog compared to the frightened and dangerous creature that came back to us. He might, eventually, perform in shows.

The moral to this little story is that damage done at the puppy stage takes a lot of undoing (if it can be undone at all) and that it needs every family member to follow the same training method.

Ill-treatment does not have to include beating or neglect – all it needs is a total lack of understanding.

Another lesson is apparent here: severe restrictive devices such as muzzles and choke chains are an admission of failure. They may make a dog cower but they won't make it well-behaved.

Frightened dogs are, more often than not, badly behaved. And frightened dogs bite.

Every time we kiss Bendi on his black nose we joke, 'Don't make eye contact!'

> *The gentle way is not only best but also quicker and much more reliable.*

I have used the dog-whispering technique on a variety of dogs, sometimes puppies, sometimes on dogs that are old enough to be settled in their ways, and more than once with extreme cases like Bendi.

Dogs communicate with each other by body language and expression. As soon as you talk to a dog in the language it uses there is an immediate understanding that speeds progress.

Can Man Speak Animal?

That is one big question!

Whenever I give a lecture I have to broach the difficult subject of talking to animals and, even worse, the possibility that animals might just talk back to me – and, even more unbelievably, the possibility that both of us might actually understand one another.

The minute I mention it I see absolute disbelief and embarrassment on the faces of my audience: 'Hello! He's raving mad.'

As soon as I press the right buttons I see the disbelievers realise that this is not madness but a lack of perception on their part.

'Does anyone have a cat?' I ask.

The hands go up.

I ask them to remember a sequence of events that they, as cat-owners, will have experienced.

It is a cold, frosty night. The cat comes through the cat-flap with its tail straight up in the air and looks intently into the eyes of its owner.

The owner knows that the cat is trying to communicate, but doesn't stop to think how daft the concept of talking cat is – they just do it. The body language of the cat asks a direct question: 'Can I have some food?' The owner, without thinking, puts some biscuits in their pet's dish.

Now, here's the clever bit. The cat, with a single look, can show that it doesn't want biscuits. This look shouts disapproval and, what's more, the owner understands and puts some meat in the other bowl.

After feeding, the cat comes to where you are sitting. It has slightly lowered its tail and is now purring. It rubs its head and body on your legs.

The communication is eloquently plain. It wants a cuddle. So, you can speak cat!

Let's try dog.

A dog slides out of the bushes. It has made its body a smaller target area. Its lips are drawn back over its teeth, its hackles are up. Its intentions are perfectly clear. It is going to bite you.

Or another scenario: the dog bounds out to see you, tail wagging so energetically that its whole body is also wagging from side to side. Its tongue is out and it is puffing happily.

It is friendly and the message is clearly a request for a fuss.

So you see, we *can* speak animal.

What I have said so far is straightforward. The body-language examples have been simple. Later in the book I will say things like 'when your dog is frightened' and though this may sound pretty obvious it isn't always.

There are unmistakable signs like flinching or cowering, but a tail held between the legs can also indicate physical discomfort such as stomach pain or, in the case of a bitch, it could mean an oncoming season.

It is a bit like a car that suddenly stops; it might be something simple like the petrol running out but it could also be caused by dozens of other things.

I am sure that a dog can communicate the subtleties of a particular kind of fear or anxiousness to another dog but it is unlikely that we will ever comprehend the specifics: it is enough that we understand the dog is unhappy. If the unhappiness persists, look harder for a likely cause.

The most important thing is to learn to really *look.*
The ability to understand is in every one of us.

We all understand more than we believe we do.

Chapter Two

Dog Teaches Man

Years ago, in Devon, I bought two sheepdog puppies. I had watched their mother working so had a fair idea of how capable they might be. At the time I worked on a farm as a shepherd and the dogs were going to work sheep.

One of the puppies seemed to be on exactly the same wavelength as me. His name is Bob. When he was around four months old I took him to see the sheep. I did not expect him to do much but hoped he might familiarise himself with the animals he, hopefully, would be working with. It was a warm day so we sat in the dappled green shade of a small wood at the edge of the sheep field.

He did something that I noticed and stored for future reference. He looked at the sheep, then looked at me, then repeated the action over and over again. I was so busy watching him that I didn't realise he was talking to me and wanted an answer.

In the end I used the same head and eye movement
he was using but reversed it, looking first at him,

27

then emphatically at the sheep, and exaggerating
the neck movement in an attempt to mirror the
way he had done it to me.

As soon as I had done this he walked towards the sheep and, over the next hour, gathered them, in twos and threes, and moved them to the other end of the field. When he had finished I stood up and walked slowly towards him. He stopped what he was doing and strolled back to me.

Anyone who has trained a sheepdog will recognise just how unusual this incident is. Young dogs will run at sheep and certainly won't come back on a mere body-language signal. The norm would be half an hour of shouting.

Bearing in mind how tiny he was, the fact that he had dared to walk towards them was surprising in itself. Usually I would not dream of asking a dog of four months to do anything, except maybe to lie down. So, this little dog was either a canine genius or I had stumbled on a new way of training. I spent the next hour telling him how clever he was by talking softly and stroking him.

This book is not about training sheepdogs but anyone who has seen what is expected of a sheepdog in a trial will immediately recognise that their own task is a lot less demanding.

The old way of training a dog concentrated on dominance: I am your master/mistress. You must do as I tell you.

Dog whispering treats the dog as a partner.
It is altogether more gentle and doesn't aim
to break the dog's spirit.

There are many commands that rely on eye contact, body language or sound. In broad terms, when the dog is close to you, use body language and eye contact; when it is far away, use sound.

So, what do you need to know?

How to make a dog

- sit

- lie down

- stop

- stand

- walk on

- stay

- walk nicely on the lead

- come back when called

- stay close when walking off the lead

You will want to stop your dog jumping up at visitors and make it a good mixer with other dogs. There will be other problems, too, like encouraging it to relieve itself in suitable places. If you live in the country or go there on holiday, you will need to make it reliable when close to sheep or cattle.

If you have not yet purchased a puppy you might like to think about what breed of dog suits the environment you live in and your lifestyle, and give some thought to a name that the dog will recognise quickly instead of something purely decorative.

If you have a rescue dog, you might need some help with training.

In the following pages I will try to give you a host of useful tips and training methods that will make life with your dog a more enjoyable and rewarding experience.

Chapter Three

The Puppy

U nless love has already conquered logic, it is wise to pick a puppy that suits your lifestyle and your energy level.

When a very large person came to buy one of my working puppies I refused to sell them one. This will sound to some like jaundiced discrimination but the question, based on observation, has to be asked: how did they become so fat?

It certainly wasn't a regime of fitness training and sensible eating that did it. The outcome then is likely to be a fat and unhappy dog that gets no exercise. And if the dog is unhappy it will come back to me with a 'no good' label hanging round its neck.

In short, it will be ruined but through no fault of its own. One difference between dogs and people is that dogs don't deceive themselves. Of course I never told the people that.

The truth is that through owners' lack of understanding, lots of dogs are ruined. Conversely, very few owners are ruined by their dogs.

Common Sense

If you live in an urban area a Springer Spaniel is probably not a good idea. If you are a jogger, a Bulldog should not be your first choice.

Take a candid look at your family and your situation and choose a breed that will suit. A Border Collie living with someone who hates exercise will turn into a snappy, furniture-eating monster, not because there is anything wrong with the dog but because it does not get sufficient opportunity to exercise both brain and body.

This is a good place to add a note about rescue dogs: whatever the breed, or the type, normal common-sense rules are naturally harder to apply. Previous history will have shaped a rescue dog's behaviour and, as you may never know what treatment your dog received before you gave it a home, you could be facing a job more suited to a psychoanalyst!

Bad dog reputations are created by people who do not know how to treat a particular breed. If a dog has been shaped by generations of work and breeding, it is not likely to change because you take a momentary shine to it.

Some dogs need their minds continually fed with challenges. If you don't have the time or inclination to do this, do not buy a dog bred to work.

The dog is not some newly arrived accident. It did not just turn up on your doorstep ready to be transformed into a member of your human family. It has evolved to fit a niche. Whether or not its recent history is known, its shaping has been going on for a very long time. Millions of years ago nature started to develop the dog according to some mysterious evolutionary plan to make it fit for purpose. Man then added his own requirements to the mix by breeding the most suitable dogs for his needs, and the breeds as we know them began to emerge.

Herding dogs were refined to do their job better. That meant they were bred to be sharper, fiercer and more energetic. Retrievers retrieve, running dogs run, fighting dogs fight, toy dogs are great for petting.

We can't take some kind of rubber or eraser and just clean off the bits in a dog's nature we don't like. Neither can we ignore the 'bred into the genes' tendencies that are strongly imprinted into certain breeds. We cannot take a dog that lives to run and, by our will, turn it into a dog that is going to sit on our lap.

What we can do is choose wisely the sort of dog that suits the way we and our family live.

If I were to tell you about the good and bad of each breed of dog this would be a very long book (there are over eighty breeds that come under A). What I can do is to offer up a kind of short-cut.

Take a good, long look at the shape of the dog you have chosen.

What it is will be apparent with closer inspection.

If it is slim, rangy and muscular it has been bred for movement, so bags of movement is what it must have. The Greyhound is a good example of this type of dog. Ideally, your physique and tendencies should be similar to its if the partnership is to be satisfying for you both.

It isn't just physical compatibility that is important. Consider also the disposition of person and dog. By nature I am always on the go, always doing this job or that, so I suit sheepdogs because they like to be busy too. A bad match would be someone who loves to sit on the sofa and read the papers, or watch television all day, owning, say, a mud-loving, energetic, restless dog like a Jack Russell Terrier.

However good the training, this blend of person and dog will never quite hit it off.

A dog will do what it is bred to do and unless you like doing the same sort of thing the relationship is unlikely to be a smooth one.

The breeds of fighting dogs that have received such bad publicity merit a mention here. Unfortunately some of the people who choose them instinctively seem to recognise the aggressive streak in the dog and this is perhaps because the same tendency exists in them. The combination of aggressive dog and potentially like-minded human is an explosive device just waiting to go off. It is a partnership made in hell which would be perfect for a job like war but has no place in a world that desires peace.

It is interesting to me to note that when someone is attacked and bitten by a fighting dog it happens most often when the owner is not there. Usually the dog has been left with the owner's mother or wife and, sensing that control has been removed, it reverts to type and attacks something, or someone, smaller and weaker than itself. By nature, this kind of dog will attempt to dominate by aggressive violence.

A saint would not be able to change the nature of a fighting dog. It is what it has been bred to be.

Nurture cannot undo nature – the best that can be hoped for is to harness what the dog is.

The choice of dog is all-important. I have owned a lot of dogs of many different breeds. My first, when I was a little boy, was a mongrel that I named Sugar Ray after the American middleweight boxer, because he too moved sweetly. The shape of his body suggested that he had a strong Cocker Spaniel streak. By nature he was nice, adoringly loyal, affectionate and brilliant with children. Cocker Spaniels make wonderful family dogs. They are not too big and do not need huge amounts of exercise: a game in the garden seems to provide as much enjoyment as a six-mile walk. They are full of fun and will fit into a family with ease and great apparent pleasure.

Springer Spaniels are different and need humans with huge reserves of energy. Springers like mud and water and brambles, especially if all three are combined. If you have a beautiful cream carpet it won't stay that way for very long with a Springer in the house. It is a country dog.

The Cocker and the Springer are gun dogs used to country living but the Cocker seems much more able to adjust to urban life. The Springer is not a good lead dog, preferring to be free range, and will show its frustration at confinement by never knowing when the game of retrieving is finished. A frustrated Springer is quite capable of driving its owner mad with its compulsive need for just one more throw.

Without training, both will quarter a field or rummage a hedgerow and send up birds as they were originally bred to do. The only disadvantage (particularly with the Cocker Spaniel) is the long ears that dangle in dinners as well as mud and can cover and flick a clean surface in seconds. If you choose a spaniel buy a deep, specially designed food bowl that will keep its ears out of the gravy.

Where there is undisturbed muck there will be germs, so for your dog's sake and yours make sure a Spaniel's ears are kept clean.

My wife and I have had four Cocker Spaniels – Tina, Penny, Sally Slapcabbage and Mandy – and I must say that they were an absolute delight. They were as good at lying peacefully by the fire as they were at searching woodlands for irresistible sniffs. Sally was so named because her favourite pastime was to pick up a cabbage leaf and shake it so violently that the slapping noise could be heard from some way off . . .

We have also had a Yellow Labrador, another Sugar Ray. It was a long time ago but my memory of him is fond. He was biddable and lovingly patient with our children, who would sit with him in his bed and even dress him up in summer bonnet and shawl. He never complained. I also remember that he pulled badly on the lead and delighted in punch-ups with other large dogs. Labrador hairs are short and curved and hold on to carpets as though it were their destiny.

If these dogs get bored they can eat their way through a wall. I discovered this when I came home from work early to show the landlord around, only to find a pile of bricks and a Labrador with his back legs in the kitchen and his head and shoulders in the living room. Eviction (or at least a good telling-off) was avoided by the judicious placing of a large settee and a quick sweep up.

Verdict: a nice dog with an even-tempered calmness and trustworthiness that suited our busy family lifestyle. But Labradors need to be kept occupied as strength and boredom are lethal companions.

For a short time we owned Prince, a Newfoundland, a great black grizzly bear of a dog. Just try bringing one back into the house after a rainy walk! Newfoundlands are famous for their swimming ability but this one couldn't swim a stroke. I had to dive into a tidal river (fully clothed in the middle of winter) to rescue him on more than one occasion. He was not as easy-going or as trustworthy as our Labrador but in fairness to him he was a rescue dog and I have no idea what he might have suffered before he came to us.

For a time, we looked after a Great Dane called Caesar. For all his size, he was frightened of the dark. I remember him as being gentle and kind with children but eating enough food to feed a small family. He was strong but walked like a lamb on the lead and could cross a crowded room without so much as nudging a piece of furniture.

At the time of writing we have fourteen Border Collies and a Sheltie: Bob, Ben, Muppet, Misty, Gemma, Fadey, Polly, Megan, Susie, Barney, Jack, Bendi, Khuni, Sally and Gem. Since I started training and breeding working sheepdogs, my wife and I have loved and lost Annie, Molly, Grumble and Wing.

The Collies are, as you would expect, motivated by work, perpetual motion machines, but their personalities range across the whole spectrum, from sweet and loving, to stand-offish and even plain irritable. They all share a highly developed ability to focus on a task and to learn new things seemingly effortlessly.

Choose a Border Collie only if you are prepared to devote a huge amount of time to feeding its demanding mind as well as its body.

Our little Sheltie, Gem, is old now and her teeth hurt, which can make her snappy if she is stroked too hard around the muzzle area.

Shelties were once called 'Tolly' dogs because their job was to guard the 'Tolly' or homestead. If sheep wandered into the vegetable garden the Tolly would run out and bark like mad to attract the sheepdogs, who would then put the 'sheepy' indiscretion right.

Shelties are like miniature 'Lassie' dogs or Rough Collies – very pretty, very lively and ideally suited to living indoors. Ours loves my wife like mad and can be found stuck to her heels for most of the time.

Gem is not only tolerant of our grandchildren but actively interested and involved with their doings. A great dog to have if you and your family live in an urban setting. Shelties also make excellent companions for older people.

As well as the dogs that I have had the pleasure of living with there are the ones that belong to relatives and friends and, of course, those I have trained.

My cousin Brian has two Shih Tzu, an ancient breed originating in China or Tibet. They are small, calm by nature and very pretty – the breed is sometimes known as the Chrysanthemum Dog because their faces resemble the flower. When I visit him I am impressed by their easy-going ways. Unlike my Border Collies the little dogs allow visitors to come and go unmolested. They are good house dogs, built for comfort rather than speed, easily trained and slot happily into family life.

Brian's dogs sleep outside his bedroom, ever watchful of his movements but never violating protocol by actually entering the room.

Friends of ours have a Staffordshire Bull Terrier. Small, solid as a teak plank, power-packed and affectionate, it doesn't know its own strength. I don't think I would choose one if there were small children living in the house. There is nothing wrong with the dog or the breed, but selective breeding has given it the most powerful jaws. My question would always be: why does it need them?

The answer is so that it can grip. Enough said.

My (doted on) grandmother had a Wire-haired Terrier called Chum and the lady next door had a Pekinese with the amazing name of Mr Woo. The Terrier's one ambition seemed to be to catch the other, which is not my idea of peaceful coexistence. So, dear as he was, no thanks.

The Pekinese, the venerable Mr Woo, on the other hand, was a delightful little thing.

You can see what a dangerous chapter this is. If I come down against a particular breed, all of its followers will be so up in arms that they will cease to read any further.

I used to see it happen when I was a vicar: say just one thing that someone did not like and they wouldn't hear the rest of the sermon – anger would overpower logic.

Butchers seldom recommend fish.

My apologies go to the owners of breeds that I have not even mentioned. They will now be jumping up and down.

In the end beauty is in the eye of the beholder and my job here is to concern myself with training not with recommending individual breeds.

But, again, do make sure that the dog you choose suits you. The initial surge of love might have to sustain itself for fifteen years or so.

Children

If you have children, especially young ones,
find a dog that is patient and calm and insist that
the children's training is thorough too.

Nothing will undo your training faster and ruin a good dog quicker than a child who has no idea how to live with it. If you love your dog you need to ensure that your children treat it well.

Sometimes people say to me, 'We always have the same breed because they suit us.' That is a good decision because over the years they have learned not only what suits them but have also stored a lot of knowledge about that particular breed, which will prove useful once training starts.

You must have heard the saying that people look like their dogs. I take that as an indication that they are well matched.

Understanding

I would never let a puppy leave its mother before the age of twelve weeks. When the mother got fed up with offering her puppies milk, I would then wean them and only when they were fully weaned would they be sold.

Most responsible breeders will try to match the puppy to the owner. If I were picking a working puppy I would want one that was bold and not one that was retiring. If I were picking a puppy to be a pet, my logic would be different.

A Good Match

When people came to see me about buying a puppy I would watch them carefully. In oversimplified terms, a big, bluff man needs a bold dog, not a timid one. A quiet, gentle, woman needs a dog to match. A lot has been written about buying the bold puppy that runs out to meet you, and there is some sense in this – but if you are quiet and retiring, take another look at the shy little dog at the back.

It can be argued that the runt of the litter should be avoided because it is smaller, and possibly weaker, than the others and may be more timid. My experience tells me that this is not always so.

The timid puppy might only be so because it is living with several forceful dogs. There is nothing worse than a noisy person who has totally intimidated a shy dog except perhaps the bold dog that has learned to intimidate the whole family.

The ideal must be when owner and dog look like a match made in heaven.

All You Need is Love

There is another way of course: you can walk into the kennel and see which one you fall in love with. There is a lot to be said for this approach, as the love will likely make you more patient when the puppy starts to show you its full nature.

Love is a great fuel to run a puppy on.

Let me state the obvious. A puppy is a baby. It does not have the wherewithal either mentally or physically to embark on a training programme until it is around six months old. It can be taught, at an early age, to use the back garden rather than the kitchen floor, but this should be done with endless patience.

Where's My Mum Gone?

Bear in mind that your puppy has been taken away from its mother and is going to be unsettled. Furthermore mother would have cleaned the puppy whenever it made a mistake.

In short, the puppy is a lost baby and your first concern should be to supply love, warmth, rest and lots of comforting. I have heard people say, 'I want this puppy to start as it means to go on', and others who believe in rubbing their puppy's nose in the mess it has made indoors. This is foolish, destructive and backward-looking mumbo jumbo that demonstrates to anyone watching that the human has a lower IQ than the dog.

This kind of treatment will do enormous harm to your puppy's development. It will result in your puppy being totally confused about what is expected of it. And this confusion will spread to every aspect of training.

The first job with a new puppy is to build a strong bond of trust.

If your puppy gets to know that you are always there for it, it will repay the compliment.

Trust is Earned

Gaining a puppy's trust is done by being soft and kind with absolute consistency. Progress can be severely checked by just one lapse into irritability.

A Puppy Needs a Routine it is Happy With

If the mother is with her puppy and it cries, she will comfort it. You need to be like the mother. Think about it: would you rather work with someone who is totally pleasant or with an ogre? There is only one answer!

Naming Your Puppy

Dog whispering starts the minute you meet your new puppy: get it used to the sound of your voice so that it looks at your face to see where the sound is coming from. This attention habit will pay huge dividends later as it will get your puppy used to looking at your face.

The first thing your puppy needs to learn is its name. Short names are best. For good reason shepherds give their dogs names like Ben, Bob, Meg, Moss.

A name like Bob is ideal because the B at the beginning and the one at the end can be emphasised to make a clear, unmistakable sound.

Giving your dog a name that is intended to impress the nearest human to you is to rather miss the functional point. A name is a tool rather than a decoration. 'Come back Descartes' might make a small point about your intellect (not necessarily the one you would want) but won't get your pup back as effectively as a name like Sam, Jack or Ben.

Chapter Four

Toilet Training

U sually, a puppy wants to relieve itself soon after eating. As it is going to start by eating four or five small meals a day, you should reckon on being on toilet duty, to begin with at least, for a fair proportion of the day.

I had trouble with Bendi when he came back to me, even as a mature dog, because he did not know where he was meant to go to the toilet. He would often hold himself until he was back in the safety of the kitchen and then do it there. When it was dark I took him out into the garden and showed him where one of the other dogs had been. He obliged by using the same spot.

A Personal Demonstration

If this had not worked I was quite prepared to give a personal demonstration – nowhere near as silly as it sounds.

If you do not have another dog then borrow one for five minutes and let it use your garden as a toilet signpost for your puppy.

Introduce the dogs to one another first so that your puppy recognises a friendly signal.

Some people put newspaper down in the kitchen so that if there is an accident it will at least happen on the paper, but this I fear initiates a wrong habit.

Your puppy is not likely to make the discovery that newspapers are for accidents only: once made, it might not be possible to break the association.

Let's be plain and straightforward about toilet training.

We humans make sense of our world by giving each place a name, and then learn the word associations and the taboos that go with them. The lavatory is suitable to use whereas the lounge isn't. A dog doesn't think like that. Add to this the fact that a puppy does it where it stands and Mother cleans it up – in the same way that a human baby would perform.

For a dog, the place deemed fit for use as a toilet is the one that smells right. So the aim is not so much to forbid one place but to encourage the use of another. Once your dog, or other dogs, have established a place, that is where all of them will go. It is up to you to make sure that the chosen spot suits you.

A puppy will eat frequently and will therefore need to relieve itself frequently. As soon as your puppy has eaten, carry it outdoors and sit it down in the area you have chosen. It will fiddle about and play but eventually the moment will come. Make a huge fuss with lots of 'Good dog, good dog' noises.

Some cotton on quickly and others don't, but the lesson will be learned if you persist.

Here are some don'ts:

- Don't rub your puppy's nose in the mess it has made. Your puppy will not connect the two things and will be alarmed and frightened to the point where it will not know whether it is coming or going.

   Remember, your puppy is a baby (and you wouldn't do it to a human baby!).

   The message needs to be clear and will not be helped by adding terror to the list of ingredients.

   It might help you to feel the satisfaction of revenge but it will make the puppy totally confused and furthermore set up barriers of fear that will hamper its ability to learn other lessons (especially when your retribution is irrational and frightening). After all, who is going to want to be taught by a violent monster?

- Don't put newspapers down in the hope that your puppy will use those rather than the floor because it sends the message that doing it on the newspapers is OK.

- Don't punish a puppy or a grown dog for doing it on the floor because they will not connect the crime with the punishment. Take them out to where you want them to go.

   If your puppy does go on the floor, clean the spot thoroughly so that all evidence is removed. If it can smell any scent remaining on the spot it will be encouraged to repeat the performance in the very same place. The lingering smell will work like a magnet and draw your puppy (and any other dog) back time and time again.

- The biggest don't is to leave your dog on its own for hours and then blame it if it messes on the floor.

You should know that when you've got to go, you've got to go!

Chapter Five

Stop and Walk

Five-minute Sessions

When your puppy is around six months old you can start the basic training. Concentrate on sessions that last no longer than five minutes and try to make them fun. On day one, do not use a lead and on day two do. The idea is to teach your puppy to walk well both on and off the lead.

Continue the on- and off-the-lead sessions for as long as it takes. Remember that a lead has an animal on each end and that both of them need to work in harmony.

The lead is no more than a connection or a conduit: it should never be used to drag or jerk the puppy.

It is important to realise that the minute a dog is put on a lead it is disadvantaged: it cannot protect itself from other dogs and it is not at all sure what your intentions are.

Patience

My wife is the best person I have ever seen at lead training; she has never, ever pulled a puppy and is prepared to stand in one spot patiently until the puppy wants to walk on and then is prepared to do it all over again when the puppy stops.

If she lead-trained a puppy it would never regard the lead as something to be frightened of. She would never use a choke chain or any kind that tightens with pulling.

Eight or so years ago I bought two puppies from a farm in North Devon and really looked forward to training them. Their background was impeccable, with grandparents who were national champions. I took great care over everything, even the choice of names: one was to be called Cariad (Welsh for 'darling'), the other Megan. Naturally their working commands would be in Welsh.

I noticed that they were both 'soft' dogs – in other words shy or timid – but figured that this was because they were young and calculated that they would both grow out of it.

In contrast my own breeding line had produced strong, confident dogs and perhaps I failed to treat these two incomers differently. I soon realised that the training with Megan was not progressing as it should. And we hadn't even reached the difficult stages.

I could not get her to walk calmly on the lead. Her behaviour suggested that I was trying to strangle her.

At the time our lives were very busy. There was the North Devon Dog Training and Breeding Centre to run, other people's dogs to train and demonstrations to worry about. I was feeling pressured and this was reflected in my impatient training of Megan.

Remembering how good my wife Maureen had been at

nurturing timid dogs I asked her to take over this stage of the training. Within two or three days the improvement was remarkable.

One day I secretly watched her training Megan to walk on the lead. It came as no great surprise to see that absolute patience was the answer.

Megan was on an ordinary clip lead and she was allowed to set the pace. There was no pulling, no hurrying, the lead stayed slack.

If an interesting sniff was found then Megan was given as much time as she wanted to enjoy it. Our lawn would have taken perhaps a minute to walk around; Maureen and her charge took close on one hour.

Then, believe it or not, they set out to do it all over again.

I could see that Megan grew calmer and more at ease with each step. Whereas, before, the lead had frightened her it now seemed to offer no terrors.

After a few days of this, Maureen handed Megan back to me along with a quiet rebuke: 'Don't be impatient!'

I can remember feeling rather insulted that she thought she could teach the trainer to train dogs but deep down realised that she was right.

The outcome of her patient approach stood directly in front of me, happily wagging a confident tail.

At best, being irritable adds time on to the training process. At worst, it destroys the dog's confidence and can prevent further progress being made.

Thinking that you know it all is like pulling the blinds down so that no light can penetrate; and if the trainer can't learn, the dog stands little chance.

I have very nearly ruined two dogs by responding too quickly and too irritably to their mistakes. My advice to you is: take your time.

When it comes to working with animals you should never reckon on doing anything that takes ten minutes in less than an hour.

Let's start without the lead. Bend down and put your hand softly on your puppy's back, look it in the eyes lovingly (with eyes wide open), stand still then say 'Stop' – no need to use the dog's name. Keep your hand on your puppy and begin to step forward very slowly, moving your body in an exaggerated way (leaning into the pace that is to come) and saying just one word: 'Walk.'

Dogs speak to each other by means of exaggerated movements of the neck and head. Stretch your neck in the direction you are travelling.

Do this exercise no more than three times in each session. At first it will not work but after a few days an understanding will develop and then suddenly it will happen.

Build One Brick at a Time

This is one of the most important lessons as walking well on the lead depends on it, as do many other parts of future training.

It is the first brick. Do not start training on another part of the programme until it works to perfection.

The next day do exactly the same thing, using a lead but always keep the lead slack.

If you feel impatience coming on, leave the session until the next day. Always end the session by making a big fuss of your puppy whether or not you have achieved any real progress.

I Sentence You to the Lead

If your puppy associates the lead with being some form of restraint, imprisonment or punishment you defeat the whole purpose. You will notice that I never advocate treats as an incentive. Treats make a dog worse, disturb its diet and are not 'on message'. If you stop to think about it, using treats is like adding another aspect to a message which is extra to the one your puppy is trying to learn. Cuddles are a much better reward and always make your dog happy.

Once your puppy is walking effortlessly on the lead, try dragging the sole of your shoe along the ground as you say, 'Stop.' Before long the dragging sound will be recognised as 'stop' – particularly useful at kerbs.

OK, six to eight months have gone by. What have you achieved? Well, you now have a dog that loves and trusts you and its confidence has no dents in it – a confident platform for further training has been built on the basis of this love and trust.

Your dog goes to the loo where you want it to and the biggest area of frustration and tension is removed.

It has learned to look at your face – and likes what it sees.

It can walk well on and off the lead, understands 'stop' and 'walk' as well as the body language that indicates both of those commands – and, perhaps even more important, you have laid the foundation for all that is to follow.

Your dog has learned to watch your body movements
as a clue to what you want it to do.

The essence of what you want your puppy to do is expressed in your face. Your puppy will take to looking at it – a sure sign that real progress is being made.

As you move on to new commands don't leave the previously covered exercises behind. Repeat them but do them after the new exercise, so that your dog always finishes its training routine with something it is totally confident about.

Don't forget to make a fuss of your dog after each session and remember: commands are single words, praise is as many as you want to use.

You will find that a bridge of understanding
will be built quickly because, with body language,
you are communicating with your dog in the
language it uses.

The Dog is Not Your Servant

A further point well worth remembering: a dog is not your servant but your partner. I have seen many trainers ruin a good dog because they were unable to visualise a relationship other than master and dog.

Have you heard the fable of the wind and the sun? The wind boasted that he could make the man below him take off his coat faster than the sun could. The sun accepted the wager. The wind blew and blew, but the man simply wrapped his coat more firmly around himself.

When the sun took its turn, all it did was shine. Soon the man was too hot and took off his coat. There is something of the dog-whispering technique in that little tale.

Chapter Six

Stand, Sit or Lie Down

The most practical of these three options is 'stand'. If the field or park you are in is muddy, or worse, then 'lie down' is not such a good choice, especially if your dog lives indoors. 'Lie down' does have advantages when the dog is a long way off because you can see that the command has been obeyed. The best thing to do is to train your dog to do two of these three things.

You should be able to see fairly quickly which of the options your dog prefers. Give them the choice: they will always do best when the choice is theirs.

Do not try to force the dog into doing something it does not want to do, unless it is something as vital as stop or stay. I have known dogs that will stand perfectly but hate lying down and vice versa. 'Sit' is something that most dogs will automatically do.

A tip: now that your dog is used to looking at your face make a point of keeping your eyes wide open.

Open eyes show you are relaxed and happy.
Eyes that are narrowed show your irritation
and possibly aggression.

So if you are displeased, narrow your eyes, hunch your shoulders, stick your neck out and stare at your dog. This should be sufficient, but if it isn't add a growled 'NO'.

Your imitation of the dog's own language will be recognised immediately. Confine this particular treatment to the puppy or the young dog.

Let me explain this important point. The most powerful dog in a pack, which can be either male or female, will use this body language to subdue a dog that is lower in the 'pecking order'. The puppy's mother will have used this method of communication, so your puppy will recognise it as normal.

As you are the pack boss it will not be unexpected. The action is a threat, to warn of a potentially more dangerous encounter, and the young dog will almost be glad that it was not more serious. Use this threat sparingly. Overuse will diminish its impact and intimidate your dog.

Sit

'Sit' is a good command word. Emphasise the ssss and attack the t at the end of the word. Your body language is all-important too.

If you are right-handed, put your dog on your left. Make it stand so close that its body is up against your legs. Now place your hand gently on its head, palm down, and walk forward just one or two paces.

Stop walking, decisively. Say 'stop', then 'sit', and push down gently on the top of the dog's head. Do not push down by force. What will happen the first time is that your dog will stop because it has already learned to do so, then it will look up at you. Still looking at your dog, put your hand on its rump and push it gently into the sit position.

If there is still confusion (and I would fully expect that), don't be afraid to bend down and arrange the dog in the exact position you want.

> *Do it gently, not roughly. It is an encouragement not a rebuke.*

If the sit happens quickly, all you have to do is to repeat the exercise. If it takes a rearrangement of limbs several times then persist. It will happen. Talk gently as you settle your dog in the required position.

Dogs usually find this manoeuvre an easy one – except, of course, a dog that doesn't find sitting normal. Try it over a week. If it has not begun to work by now, think about the possibility that your dog does not like sitting. I have a dog with a hip problem and sitting is something it cannot manage with the best will in the world.

A more natural way to achieve this is to stand and talk to a neighbour, especially if they have a dog with them. As you talk, keep your eye on your dog. Ten to one, it will sit of its own accord.

If this happens, still say 'sit', even if it comes after the dog has sat down, and follow this with much praise.

Lie Down

Just like 'sit', but you will need to bend down and arrange your dog's position certainly for the first few attempts. Do not shorten the command to 'down': 'down' will have a quite different meaning later in the training programme. Instead, put emphasis on the word 'down' so that there is a memorable link with other commands that also contain 'down'.

Do not be tempted to bark commands like a sergeant major: save the loud voice for when you need it. Remember that you are your dog's reliable and kind friend.

If you save the shout for when it is really needed, it will have all the impact and shock value you could possibly hope for. If shouting becomes the norm then your dog will only ever obey a shout and you will have thrown away the opportunity to register a real emergency.

Keep Them Close

Throughout all of this stage of the training it pays dividends to keep your dog touching your leg. It won't take long for it to 'read' the movement of your leg and complete the manoeuvre without the spoken command.

The sequence of training sessions that I have chosen has yielded near perfect results for me time and time again.

Long experience with all sorts of dogs has shown that there is an enormous benefit to be had by thoroughly training a dog close up, as memory of the facial expressions and body language (unnoticed by us) seems to lodge firmly in the dog's mind and undoubtedly aid its understanding when it is working at a distance.

Therefore, the benefits of scrupulous close work are manifold and far reaching.

Just One Trainer

Do not be tempted to let someone else take over the training if you can't make it. It is always best to avoid confusion in the dog's mind by keeping to just one trainer even if you miss some sessions.

That is not to say that the dog will never obey anyone else. At the very end of the training someone else can take over but only if you teach them precisely how to do it. And I do mean precisely!

Causing Confusion

I have listened to couples both barking out different orders to their dog and then agreeing that the dog is disobedient. You both have to use the same words and the same body language.

I have seen really good dogs on farms fall apart when someone else tries to work them.

Dog whispering starts and finishes with understanding and, however good the dog might be, if you don't try to understand what it is thinking you stand no chance at all of succeeding.

Some shepherds working a brace of dogs speak to one in English and one in Welsh. I work nine dogs at the same time and use nine different languages. Even after a demonstration where this has been explained fully, an allegedly professional trainer will ask my Welsh dog to sit using the English command. They then look amazed when the dog ignores them completely.

If something is slowing your progress, look at yourself before you look at your dog.

Stand

If the dog prefers 'stand' to 'lie down' or 'sit', it will show signs of the preference almost from the outset of this stage in the training. If this is the case then you are lucky because you can miss a whole session. 'Stand' can also mean 'stay' but we shall come on to that in due course.

Chapter Seven

The Bridge

This next exercise builds a bridge between controlling your dog at your feet and when it is some distance away.

It is a must for every dog owner exercising their dog in an open space.

A Pleasing Result

Several things happen at this point and some are quite noticeable. At the start your dog, maybe a touch reluctantly, did as you asked because it knew it was pleasing you.

Now you will see that your dog is beginning to enjoy itself and the reason is because it has a body and a brain and both of these need satisfying. A lot of dogs have their bodies well fed while their brains are neglected.

Your dog is going to gain more and more satisfaction.
A lot of behavioural problems stem from owners failing
to notice that their dog needs mental stimulation.

When you have finished one of these sessions, with some kind of pleasing result, you should notice that friend dog is tired, much more at ease, and that a new confidence is apparent.

You will also see a new willingness in the pack-boss-and-pack-member relationship.

The Invisible String

Because I worked in a theme park visited by thousands of people each day, sometimes with their dogs, I wanted to be sure that I could take several dogs to and from demonstrations without worrying about their behaviour.

I practised in a quiet field and searched hard for a good way to do it. I had noticed, during demonstrations, that a younger dog would often follow an older one with a kind of military precision – almost a dog version of slow marching.

Furthermore, a dog on an opposite flank would mirror what was going on by matching its stride to the already matched pair.

It was quite spectacular: the following dog would match the other, stride for stride, pause for pause, as though they were joined together by an invisible string. Their walk looked for all the world like the well-schooled movement of a dressage horse, a sort of synchronised, deliberate perfection.

I realised that in some way a communication between the two

dogs was happening. Neither made a sound so it had to be purely by body language.

What was actually happening was that the younger, junior dog was imitating every movement of the older dog, so by deduction I realised that as my dogs see me as part of the pack – an older dog – if I did something, they would too. So, no difficult human words to understand, just instant communication.

Perhaps even more important, they obviously enjoyed the whole process. The intent look on their faces showed just how willingly absorbed they were in the process they had invented.

Their body language was noticeable: each dog's neck and head were stretched in a kind of pointing action; the mouth was shut and the eyes wide open. There was also an expression of total concentration on their faces.

I had not taught them – they were teaching me. They were also saying something quite surprising: their concentration was self-induced. I decided to teach every one of them to walk slowly either on their own or in company.

What does this mean for you? It will enable you to keep a dog near or to allow more distance between you both while retaining an unbelievable control. Linked to the other commands already learned it will mean that control of your dog off the lead will actually be better than when it is on the lead.

How does this rank in terms of difficulty? Well, it is not as hard as some of the exercises you have already performed – especially given that it is a progression from what you have done, rather than a brand-new thing.

Walk Slowly

The starting point is one that by now you are used to. Put your dog against your leg so that you can feel each other. You will be walking side by side.

Even if you are slightly behind your dog it will still be able to recognise your actions. Ideally, it should look up at your face but don't worry unduly if that doesn't happen straight away.

Now, stretch your neck out in the direction you are going and walk just one stride (a private space might be a good idea otherwise your neighbours might think that the strange walk indicates affliction).

Either by feeling your leg move or by watching your face (or both), your dog will begin to understand that you are walking forward. At the beginning it will have no idea how far or how fast. Don't worry – that will come.

What is likely to happen at the start is that your dog will overstate by walking one fairly neat step, then running. Come back and try it again, and again. But do not do more than five minutes on each session to avoid overtaxing your dog.

Pat your leg or hold out your arms in welcome to encourage your dog to come back each time. If it does not go far away from you this will indicate its level of enjoyment.

You should see a short-lived semblance of understanding fairly quickly.

What you are trying to do, in true dog-whispering style, is to get the dog to imitate your action.

Sometimes this exercise will work better on a hard surface

because you can drag the sole of your foot along the ground to give emphasis to the 'stop'.

It is a game of patience but after repeated tries you should see progress.

You can talk to your dog while you are doing it. Repeating 'one' to match the single stride you take can make the concept clearer to the dog. Saying 'slowly' with each stride will aid your ability to hold the dog back.

You can put your hand gently on the dog's back to steady it. Or even curl your hand loosely round its collar (but this impedes its ability to move forward smoothly).

How long this takes to perfect will depend on the dog and on the clarity of your intention. If I dedicated myself to it, using just one session a day, I'd need about two weeks to achieve three or four steps.

The aim is to be able to walk around ten steps with you and your dog virtually synchronised.

Once it starts to happen in a pleasing way and you are reasonably happy that the exercise is understood, take your hand off the dog's back and straighten up a little – you'll need to by now!

In very gradual stages move a little further away from your dog each day so that it goes through the exercise, without contact, at greater and greater distances from you.

An excitable dog might try to nip your coat during this process. It's a good sign if this happens because it shows both a degree of frustration *and* great interest.

If it does do this, a growled 'NO', accompanied by a facial grimace with narrowed eyes, should do the trick, but do not be tempted to growl right into the dog's face. Stop the session if the coat-nipping happens more than once during the lesson and start again next day.

Prevention Rather Than Cure

Eventually, using what you have just learned, plus the previous lessons, your dog will be attached to you because it wants to be – because it is fun to be attached to you. Friends will say that they have never seen a dog that watches its owner so intently – as though this happened by good fortune.

The next stage represents another bridge, or layer, in the training process. What you have done so far has been about prevention rather than cure.

A lot of misadventures that happen to owners of untrained dogs will not happen to you because the training you have undertaken will have anticipated the possibility of the misadventures happening.

As a for instance, a dog that runs away does so because whatever it saw to tempt it was more exciting than staying with its owner. But as your dog now sees you as the provider of ample interest and excitement, the likelihood of its running off is much reduced. Besides which, you now have a small battery of commands to arrest your dog's flight should it suddenly take off.

The critical point in stopping a dog from running away is when the thought first comes into its mind. When your dog is three miles away, it's more a case of closing the stable door after the horse has bolted.

I build layers of command when I train one of my dogs:

• by body language

- by body language and the spoken word

- by body language, word and whistle

When I have finished the dog understands the connection between each layer and, as a result, a whistled 'lie down' at a mile away works every bit as effectively as the body language used when close up. You could ask why I bother about the layers – why not go straight for the ultimate signal?

In answer, I would point out that by using layers the dog not only learns much quicker but has a complete understanding at the end of its training. Like a child doing simple sums first.

Don't forget my earlier tip which is to practise all of the sessions, always ending with the one the dog finds easiest.

Practice makes perfect. Because of the layer method, when your dog gets older it will only need a periodic reminder to recall its training.

Annie, one of my best dogs, had a stroke when she got older and overnight completely forgot the man-made parts of her training but always remembered the body-language signs. I was glad I had taken the trouble to use my layer method: it gave me more options and she had the comfort and security in her old age of knowing where I was and still understanding what I wanted her to do.

Do remember: the most important part of every stage of the training is an even-tempered kindness.

Chapter Eight

The Whistle

A sheepdog whistle is a piece of folded metal, plastic or even buffalo horn and is designed to go inside the mouth. In the centre there is a hole that goes right the way through.

It is much more effective than the traditional whistle because it can, by mouth alone, be made to make a huge variety of sounds and the volume can be controlled to produce a sound that will travel well over a mile or gently communicate with your dog when it is much closer to you.

The traditional 'pea' whistle, which is easy to blow, just produces blasts of sound with no subtlety whatsoever.

Some people can whistle by putting their fingers in their mouth and the sound comes naturally: a technique I have never mastered.

I like the sheepdog whistle for several reasons: prime among them is that if you are angry because your dog won't come, the whistle doesn't carry any hint of your mental state. It sends an emotionless and clear instruction and therefore cannot put the dog off because it senses your mood is not good.

Another reason for my liking the sheepdog whistle is that it allows the shepherd to 'talk' to his dog even though it might be a mile away.

Some people say that they are not easy to master but I found it straightforward. If you find it difficult, persevere. It does get easier and the results are certainly worth the effort.

Put the whistle into your mouth with the slightly curved side going in first; the tab, where the lanyard attaches to it, should be in line with the front of your mouth.

Hold the whistle with your lips, *not your teeth*!

Close your lips over the whistle so that you can feel the surface all the way round. The shape indicates where your lips should be.

Now, very gently, blow. The tip of your tongue should be resting on the back of the whistle. The air has nowhere to go now except through the hole in the centre of the whistle.

If you do it gently there will, after a few attempts, be a small sound. Don't be overconfident and try to produce a loud whistle (volume can come later).

My tip would be to try for just a few minutes each day and gradually success will come.

You can make different sounds by putting the tip of your tongue in different positions on the back of the whistle.

A fine way to practise is to play a tune: the accuracy needed to 'play' the music in whistle form will enable you to reproduce the same sound over and over again when it comes to dog commands.

I found that if I frowned I produced a low sound, and if I smiled a high sound.

A sheepdog whistle would be really useful in a park as your dog would have no doubt about the fact that you were calling it. The whistles can be obtained online from www.colliewobbles.org.uk.

They have a really huge variety and also sell lanyards to put the whistle on as well as tapes and CDs that suggest command calls.

Calls can be whatever you want them to be. Every shepherd picks his own.

If you would like to hear some of the calls I use, go to my website www.graemesims.com. There is also an example of sung commands.

If you intend to use a sheepdog whistle and have more than one dog, here's a tip: give each a different sound but use just one for 'come back', which applies to all. In an emergency it will be much more efficient to have just one 'come back' signal.

Remember, though, that you should only teach one dog at a time.

Trying to teach two how to understand whistle commands, at the same time, will just confuse them. Once they understand they can run together.

Finally, two useful tips:

- Use the lanyard: it will save you losing a whistle a day.

- Don't run with the whistle in your mouth unless you plan on whistling rather than talking for a while!

Chapter Nine

Working at a Distance

A shepherd must be able to work his dog precisely when it is a mile or more away in order to control the sheep. He, or she, will have trained the dog to work at ever-increasing distances until it works as well far away as it does close up. For the shepherd, the whistled command replaces the shouted command for the sake of clarity and reach.

As I've already said, another advantage of the whistled command is that it is totally without emotion.

There is no such thing as an angry whistle.

Dogs know that they can run much faster than you can so it would be foolish to try to work them at the ultimate distance to start with. A look of pure delight will cross your dog's face when it realises it is too far away for you to do much about it. This is where trouble starts.

If you start with small distances and gradually increase them, the dog never seems to grasp that it is beyond your area of control and, perhaps more significantly, does not seem to want to be outside your control.

Freedom Means Contentment

A dog really does need to run free. A long walk with your dog on the lead might satisfy you but a long meander is not much use at all to an animal designed to run.

A walk lasting an hour and a half on a lead is of less value to a dog than ten minutes' free running. If your dog is content and physically tired it will behave well. A frustrated dog won't!

You need to satisfy your dog both physically and mentally: running looks after the physical needs and challenging commands stimulate it mentally. Result – one happy and well-behaved dog.

But you also need the reassurance of knowing that you can control your dog when it is off the lead in an open space. There will be reasons other than just worrying that your dog is about to make a break for freedom.

Imagine that your dog is a hundred yards away from you when it spots a nicely decomposing bird or rabbit on the ground right under its nose. If its find is really smelly the dog will roll on it until it has spread as much of the disgusting thing as far over its body as is possible.

This is pure delight to a dog. If the deceased is only mildly rotten it will attempt to eat it, which is dangerous because of the bones that might make your dog choke, or worse. Just why they do it is explained later in the book.

Imagine now that your training programme has anticipated such a problem, that you can stop your dog in its tracks before it rolls on or eats the rotting carcass and you can call your dog back to you.

If the field or park you use for exercising your dog is bordered by a busy road you will of course need to be able to maintain control even at a considerable distance.

Chapter Ten

Come Back

'Come back' is the most important distance command. It is fairly easy to teach, providing you allow your dog to concentrate on it.

Take your dog off its lead. The wonderful smells will make it wander away from you. It doesn't matter if the distance is only a few feet.

Bend down, pat your leg and say, in your friendliest voice, 'Come back.'

Say it as if it were the most exciting thing you could say. Your dog will pick up on the tone long before it understands the words.

Strictly speaking the word 'come' is enough, but as the dog is in front of you it makes sense to include 'back'. Use 'come' on its own when your dog is lagging behind and you want it to catch up. Dogs can grasp the meaning of 'back'.

There is a whole variety of body-language signs and spoken commands that can be used. Because I work lots of dogs at the same time I tend to just call out the name of the dog I want to come to me.

Bending forward, in a non-threatening manner, is always a good idea and patting your leg always seems to be understood by the dog.

Be Welcoming

Reduce your height by stooping down so that your shape is less dominating to the dog. A shy or timid dog will respond to the stooping technique quite dramatically. If it has failed to come back half a dozen times when you are upright, the stooped (or kneeling) position will change the dog's attitude and make it far more relaxed about the whole thing.

You can hold out your arms welcomingly. Make the signal as exciting as you can because by now your dog can read your body language as easily as we read a book.

Do not keep a pocket full of tempting snacks to help you out if your dog does not respond. It will only spend more time worrying about how to get them than it does learning.

Tasty titbits are used by people who can't find any other way of training their dog and the dog will never learn the satisfaction so key to understanding that it just did something really well. All you will achieve is to teach the dog to eat food it really doesn't need.

Using a ball or a solid rubber ring might seem like a good idea because playing with it is exciting for the dog. Throwing one or the other will certainly encourage your dog to bring it back as well as helping you teach it to drop on command – useful when it picks up something forbidden. But do not let the ball or ring become a mainstay of the training programme.

If you do, you will find it encourages your dog to pick up sticks when no ball is available. Sticks are truly dangerous to a dog because they splinter or can get wedged in its mouth. A springy twig can get rammed between a dog's teeth and cause all sorts of discomfort before it is discovered.

Sticks should be avoided at all times.

I have employed both a ball and a rubber ring, but have stopped using them once the lesson has been learned.

For pure fun and exercise a rubber ring and a sufficiently large ball are great for enhancing enjoyment on a walk and both will keep your dog near you when you want it to stay close.

A word of caution, though: don't throw either for your dog when another dog is nearby, as rushing to get to it is an effortless way to start a fight that can soon become serious.

Once you have both mastered the come-back manoeuvre to the extent that it works every time, even at distance, try popping in a 'stand', 'sit' or 'lie down', reinforced by a hand held out with palm towards the dog. Do this in as military a way as you can manage so that the movement is decisive and the dog can clearly see what your intention is.

If you have practised all of the close-up exercises, you will find that your dog has become really responsive at a distance and, furthermore, now regards being out with you as the most exciting prospect imaginable.

Dogs just love to do a job well. You will see from their expression how satisfying they find it. Remember, though, that each training session should last no longer than five minutes for a puppy and no more than ten for an adult dog.

Give them plenty of time to enjoy what dogs love to do or they will become too much like robots.

Whistled Commands

The whistle is ideal for attracting a dog's attention, especially one that has seen potential canine playmates on a distant horizon and is intent on joining them. It will arrest the intention to run away more effectively than any other signal. For the pet owner wanting a very well-behaved dog, I would recommend confining whistled commands to 'stop' and 'come back'.

Make use of the same system of layers, to build bridges in the dog's understanding, that we have used so far in the training programme.

Let's use 'come back' as a demonstration of how it is done.

Your dog is perhaps ten feet away from you. Lean forward, stooping slightly, call 'Come back', pat your leg enthusiastically, then blow the whistle with the signal you have chosen. I recommend using two short whistles for 'come back', one for each word of the command. It will not be long before your dog recognises the meaning of the request.

Alternatively, break the command into two parts. First, call and pat your leg, then after several attempts using this method, add the whistled command. Both methods will work but which works best will be made clear by your dog's response.

After doing this enough times to achieve success, try just one component of the exercise. In time your dog will recognise each piece of the layer as the complete command. It will not be necessary to use body language, spoken command *and* whistled command beyond the learning process.

I realised, when writing this, that it sounds both improbable and over-complicated. The aim is that once your dog has been taught the exercise you will have three options for getting it to come back to you. When it is close, just pat your leg; at middle distance, use the voice command; and, when it is some way off, use the whistle.

It will pay you also to have a whistle signal for 'stop'. The purpose of this is to simply arrest your dog's flight, to make it stop and look back.

One harsh blast of the whistle will work well but only teach your dog to respond to this once it is totally at home with the 'come back' signals, to avoid any possible confusion between the two commands.

I repeat my earlier point that sessions should only last a few minutes. Each lesson should be regarded as a component in the total building programme. Don't move on to another 'brick' until the last one is totally understood by your dog.

At this point in the training programme, it will not hurt to give your dog three short lessons a day by joining up some of the sessions logically. As a for instance, it will benefit your dog to combine 'stop' and 'come back' as this is how they will be used in a real situation.

I Am Going to Run Away

From long and careful observation I have noticed that a dog that is about to run away goes through three stages:

- It sees, hears or smells something interesting in the distance

- It starts to move slowly towards the interest point but with no formed intention

- It makes its move, and because it runs so quickly the ever-growing intention becomes more resolute and harder to break with every passing stride

To be successful, at the beginning of training, you must arrest that flight by the second stage – before the intention is formed.

A dog that has been thoroughly trained for some time can be stopped even when it is in full flight but a learner might well find the excitement of the chase greater than the attraction of the command.

The ultimate aim of this system is to provide you with such a range of options that drifting beyond the point of no return does not even come into the equation.

Time for an aside:

I noticed only recently that there is a finite number of dogs that one person can keep under control. A photographer friend was coming to take pictures of my dogs working and asked if we could have the whole lot out of their kennels. I am used to working nine at the same time but have fourteen altogether. Once they were all out, I only just managed to control them.

There is a point at which a large number of dogs will revert to pack mentality, when no amount of training will keep them properly in order. The voice of a human becomes less meaningful than the call of the pack.

This is relevant in the context of working at a distance should you meet several dogs at the same time. With my dogs (who all know each other) it took fourteen. With strange dogs it could take as few as six or seven to blow away any chance of control.

I have had dogs that took to training like ducks to water. Others found it really difficult and only persistence and a degree of invention, plus empathy, got them there in the end. The slow learners ended up as first-class dogs.

And then I have had the rare dog that learned the process so effortlessly that it seemed as though it was teaching me.

Chapter Eleven

Does Your Dog Understand Every Word You Say?

Sometimes I hear people say that their dog knows the time or recognises the music at the end of a TV programme. 'My dog understands every word I say' is an oft-used statement by owners.

I don't believe it does. In fact, to be blunt, it certainly doesn't!

What happens is that because you recognise the theme music and know that it means time to go to bed or whatever, you lean forward or tense up or perhaps make a sound, or say something. Maybe you yawn and stretch; maybe it's as simple as picking up a coffee cup.

The music is your signal and your reaction to it is the dog's signal.

It probably all happens so automatically that you do not notice that you are doing it, but you will do the same thing every time.

Body Language

Your dog is far more adept at reading body language than you are and that is why it gets up and runs to the door – which is amazingly clever because, whatever the signal means, you are going through that door. Even if there are two doors, habit will make you use just one.

As dogs 'talk' and judge situations by body-language signs they will recognise the most subtle change in yours.

Sometimes when people are about to leave to go on holiday they notice that their dog is unsettled. This is not because the cases are being packed but because the rhythm of their body language has changed. A suitcase does not start a chain of thought in your dog: 'Ah, suitcase equals holiday equals kennels.' The dog becomes unsettled because you are unsettled.

When I go out I always say to my dogs, 'Won't be long', not because they understand the language but because I am trying to build a pattern of routine that will not unsettle them.

It is not so much that I say something, but the tone of voice I use to say it – the calm, matter-of-fact way of delivering a body-language communication that really means, 'Don't worry, everything is as it is meant to be.'

What is So Special About Sunday?

I am a minister as well as a dog trainer so on Sundays I go to church. I am always surprised that the dogs are restrained: they don't jump up or rub their hairy bodies on my best dark suit.

It would be easy to fool myself into believing that my clever dogs know that it is Sunday and that best suits must not be made hairy. Come to think of it, I am not conscious of ever having to teach or remind the dogs that Sunday is different from any other day.

They know it is different because the clothes I am wearing do not smell of the fields. They also recognise that the routine is quite different on Sundays. Different time, different pace, different body language.

At first their recognition of Sunday puzzled me. I still pick up the car keys but I don't rattle them ostentatiously – they are slipped, as silently as possible, into a quiet pocket.

I also do something else that they probably notice: I look back and 'bark' the same signal to my wife, 'See you there, dear.'

I am not looking at them invitingly, as I would do on Monday, but looking behind me and ignoring them.

So I have sent several fairly obvious signals that the dogs understand. It is the difference in pattern that they recognise and they are remarkably good at it.

A Different Intelligence

I remember a tourist to Devon asking me if sheep were stupid. When I answered that they are the cleverest animals in the world at being sheep, she looked puzzled and unsatisfied by what might have seemed a glib answer.

Actually, it was quite a good answer because sheep are wonderfully equipped to live as sheep – they have the intelligence to succeed as sheep.

Maybe the woman was comparing sheep to humans.

I can remember a bank manager at a wildlife lecture saying something similar; in so much as he thought gorillas were not too bright. I think the gorilla might make a bit of a mess in a bank but would it be any worse than the bank manager's attempt to survive in a rainforest?

Does chalk taste as good as cheese? No, of course it doesn't – but try drawing on a blackboard with a piece of cheese. Each to its own, never to be compared. Simply a different intelligence.

A dog has all sorts of abilities that we do not have but being an imitation human is not one of them. Most of the training methods that fail do so because of this basic misunderstanding.

The Wrong Signals

If you watch dog owners and their dogs you will notice that excitable people have excitable dogs, and vice versa. This is because the dog mirrors the body language of its owner just as it would do with a pack boss.

After making a real mess of one of my first demonstrations I went to see an expert for some much-needed advice. As we walked up to his farmhouse I noticed that he was watching me and my dog with a keen, comparing interest.

He made his judgement swiftly and said, 'Leave your dog in the barn because there's nothing wrong with her.'

Then he took me to the training field where, for the next hour, he taught me how to move slowly and calmly. 'You're waving your arms like a windmill. No wonder your dog is overexcited.'

The next week the new calm me tried again, and this time did very well indeed.

Overexcitement is communicated to a dog by body language and the dog responds by reading urgency into the situation and doing everything in a rush.

Often at shows I make a big point of demonstrating just how effective silent body language is. Bear in mind that I might well be working with eight or nine dogs and ten thousand people will be watching, so there is a lot of distracting noise.

If I turn and walk, the dogs turn and walk with me. It works every time and their reaction is immediate.

Crime and Punishment

Some signals, like anger, are clear to a dog, although of course it will not know why you are angry.

I do not think that a dog can link crime to punishment. You must have heard of dog owners who whack their dog with a rolled-up newspaper. They do it out of misplaced consideration. The newspaper is soft so won't hurt the dog; therefore it is not unkind. They reason that the noise it makes is useful as emphasis.

The dog's view of this treatment will be absolute puzzlement. Their normally sane owner, for no understandable reason, suddenly rolls up a newspaper and strikes poor dog.

If you meet a neighbour holding a newspaper don't be surprised if the dog tries to run away or shows signs of aggression. After all, it was the human who taught the dog what newspapers are really for.

Can you imagine living with a partner who, for no reason whatsoever, repeatedly strikes you with a weapon?

The newspaper is more frightening and unpredictable to the dog than an object that is clearly a weapon. A stick, yes, sure, that looks like a weapon. But a newspaper?

It would not be beyond the possible for my master or mistress to whack me with the remote control . . . a saucepan . . . the list of options goes on. The outcome is that anything a human picks up might just be a weapon in disguise.

Can you see the confusion in the dog's mind?

The point is that the dog cannot see a reason so cannot make a link between crime and punishment.

A Different Interpretation

Some signs say to a dog exactly the opposite of what we want them to say. The dog that runs away in the park is too often chased by its owner, who continually shouts, 'Come back! Come back!'

The dog interprets this in a totally different way and believes that because its owner is both running and 'barking', the game must be an exceedingly good one.

Therefore to prolong such a good thing must be pleasing to both of them.

You can see where the frustrations begin!

Sadly we talk to dogs in the way that we talk to foreigners. Say it loud, slowly and clearly and surely they will understand. Of course they don't, because they don't speak our language and we don't speak theirs.

Facial Expressions and Tone of Voice

If you say 'Christmas pudding' in a kind, calm voice your dog will be happy; if you say the same words fiercely, it will be concerned. As you spoke each your face changed, once to represent calm and again to represent sternness.

In time the dog learns to respond to commands and recognises its name, but whether this means it understands actual words is something that even after a lot of experience I would not be prepared to swear to.

This is Where Dog Whispering Begins

It doesn't happen instantly but over time your dog will come to understand your demeanour in a general sense from the expression on your face and the normal or otherwise movement of your body. More important, you will begin to understand your dog and realise that you can get it to do things you would not have thought possible by simple body language.

Specific commands will begin to have meaning by association. Eventually the body language will not be needed and the word alone will bring the correct response.

When a dog is commanded by whistle, it responds to the memory of the teaching layers of body language, spoken command and then whistle.

As the whistle is just a sound that does not contain any language you can see how this must be so.

Specific instructions will be understood through repetition and sympathetic body language that mirrors the dog's own language.

Warning Signs

I have a friend who walks rather awkwardly; I understand why he does so but my dogs see him as a rather dangerous animal.

His body language is not what they recognise as normal. They think that because his shoulders are raised he is bound to be aggressive. If a dog raises its shoulder muscles it is probably preparing to bite. Why should humans be any different?

For the same reason dogs often see children as a threat, especially when they make sudden, jerky movements and call out in high-pitched, excited voices.

In both the case of my slightly disabled friend and the running children, dogs make a quite different interpretation of what is happening and see them as dangerous because they are 'reading' the body language which they definitely understand as threatening.

I can remember a neighbour who happened to be photocopying in my study at dog feeding time. I told him not to go out into the garden when the dogs were eating. I stressed the point as forcefully as I could. His expression told me all I needed to know: he was not taking my recommendation seriously. He knew better. The fact that I was a dog trainer and he wasn't obviously did not carry any weight with him.

In the end he did precisely what he had been advised not to do, with the result that he very quickly ended up with a dog swinging by its teeth from his backside.

Dogs can recognise at a glance what sort of person you are and what your attitude is towards them.

His attitude towards dogs was one that I knew they would not find friendly.

My point in telling this little story is that this was a stranger and their reaction was predictable. But what if your dog can detect a similar attitude in you? What happens to your relationship if you are less than committed, or bored, or not really putting your whole mind to the task in hand? Dogs can discern the difference.

A gentle dog, perhaps brimming with talent, can be easily squashed by an over-authoritative human.

Dog whispering is holistic. You need to be sensitive and to realise that in some areas your dog knows more than you do – like distinguishing between friend and enemy – but in others it needs a lot of help and understanding to grasp what your training intention is.

Another friend is a gamekeeper and has five dogs of his own. Sometimes when I am training my dogs in the field he will open the gate and walk straight in. Some of the dogs will run towards him with tails wagging like mad; the others will look up from their work, give a quick wag and carry on.

He hasn't said anything. He hasn't done anything but his body language, his demeanour, clearly says, 'I'm your friend.'

One thing I have noticed is that, in the main, he will ignore them until they greet him. He is a man who cares about dogs, who has compassion for them and sympathy. The dog is in thrall to the human, under his dominion. It is a wise trainer who sees this with sufficient understanding to make that dominance intelligent, sympathetic and, of course, productive.

Pleasing the Pack Boss

It isn't natural for a dog to perform a series of human commands and that is why, initially, it can be a struggle.

In the dog's mind there is no sensible reason for doing all of these things but it learns that doing them pleases you and, later, discovers that it is fun.

> *Your dog tries to please you because it recognises your status in the pack.*

Pleasing the pack boss is all-important to a dog because the pack boss is stronger and cleverer than the pack member. 'Please the pack boss and you survive' might be the way the dog views it in the wild. And, as far as the dog is concerned, this is the wild.

So far in this chapter I have largely concentrated on the dog understanding the human but what about the other way round?

Can I Really Speak Dog?

If I claimed I could talk dog fluently I would be lying. I do, though, understand a lot of what they are saying because I watch them all the time.

A dog standing a couple of yards away from me with its head up, tail raised, mouth slightly open and eyes wide, looking straight into mine, is waiting with joyful expectation: 'What are we going to do next?'

Exactly the same position but with mouth shut means: 'I'm waiting but I'm not sure what you're going to do or whether I'll like it.'

A dog that keeps bending its body and slinking around you in circles is looking for reassurance. It is highly likely that it believes you are displeased and it has no way of knowing how long your displeasure might last.

A word of reassurance should follow a rebuke.

Some of the attention-seeking signs like mouthing or pawing worry many behaviourists and dog trainers but do not concern me at all because the dog is being attentive.

The hardest to deal with is a bored dog that does not want to join in with any of the training routines.

I have one little dog who steadfastly refuses to involve herself in anything that might resemble work. Even as a puppy her unwillingness was clearly communicated to me.

I have contented myself with teaching her just the basics but strangely she has managed to learn all that is needed from my other dogs.

115

*You can take the 'madness' out but you
cannot put the 'willingness' in.*

A Dog and Cat's Life

Dogs chase cats because their owners either encouraged them or, more likely, did not discourage it.

On the farms where I started my work, kittens and puppies were often born at the same time, sometimes in the same barn. They lived in a wonderful harmony, which I noticed because I was brought up in London. The farmer probably took it for granted as the norm because it had happened all his life.

I had a big tabby cat called Sam, who would leave our cottage every morning to go and catch rats in the barns.

As he entered the farmyard the two dogs, who belonged to the farmer, would stroll towards him, tails wagging like mad. There would be an exchange of nose sniffing and Sam would rub his body against the dogs. Then cat and dogs would go off to work in different directions.

This routine was a fixture of each day. So the saying 'A cat and dog's life' probably has a different meaning from the one most of us understand.

I have even had dogs and cats that would take it in turns to look after each other's babies. Pips, a beautiful tortoiseshell cat, had her kittens in her bed in our cottage. When she wanted to go out she would walk across the room and look at Annie, our first sheepdog. Annie would get up, walk over to the cat bed and gently wriggle her way in among the kittens. Only when they were settled would Pips pop out of the cat-flap.

Twenty minutes later she would return and look at Annie again, and Annie, somewhat reluctantly, would go back to her own bed.

If your dog suddenly sees a cat, say, 'NO!' Complete the instruction with appropriate body language: shoulders raised, face in a grimace and instruction delivered with a touch of venom.

It is likely that someone who owns a cat-chasing dog will argue strongly that this is normal behaviour. It is perhaps easier than admitting they have done nothing to stop it.

My dogs are not allowed to chase cats, squirrels, rabbits or any small, fast-moving furry or feathered creature.

If your dog does chase any of the aforementioned creatures and they run across a road, it will be pot luck as to which one is run over.

Car Travel

I have heard people say that their dog hates riding in cars as though the dislike was imprinted in its genes. If your dog doesn't like cars this is probably due to your approach in training.

In the case of an older dog, perhaps something happened to it when it was a puppy. Unfortunately, no amount of re-education is likely to rid the dog of its entrenched fear.

My wife developed a great method for overcoming our young dog Barney's fear of car travel.

She would open the back door of the car while she was cleaning it and let him climb in and out. Every now and then she would get into the stationary car and invite him to come in with her. They would sit together for a few minutes, then get out again. She repeated this many times. Then she would drive the car a little way with him inside it. Now he is a great traveller.

If something that the dog dislikes happens at the beginning of its career the scar is disproportionate and makes a real impression that is very difficult to overcome.

I bought a young bitch called Molly who was truly wonderful as a working dog but she would sit in the car and try to savage each oncoming vehicle. The continual snapping and rapid head-turning was deeply annoying and most unsettling.

Looking back I had purchased her when she was around six months old from a quiet moorland farm. The farmer did not look like the kind of man who would bother to keep records, so maybe she was even older. I had no way of knowing whether she had experienced something offputting before I had her or whether her introduction to the car had come a little late in the growing-up process.

When she had her first puppies I put her and them into a big, straw-filled cardboard box to take them seventeen miles each way to the theme park where I worked. There was no barking or snapping, just a wonderful silence.

There could be two reasons for this. One could be that she had her puppies to look after and the importance of this outranked any other task. Or, it could have been that the vehicle was a van, without rear windows, which prevented her from seeing the oncoming traffic.

After the puppies had grown up I let her travel with two other dogs in the rear of the car. The snapping stopped once we had been travelling for five minutes.

It took a long, long time to improve matters. I am sure that if I had been able to introduce her to car travel as a twelve-week-old puppy the problem would not have developed. Or if it had, my wife's patient method of introducing her to the inside of a stationary car would have worked.

The moral of this story is to get your puppy used to the car from the outset. Once a bad habit becomes entrenched it is exceedingly hard to break.

It helps to make sure that there is a worthwhile reward at the end of a short journey. If the dog knows that a five-minute drive will be followed by half an hour's run then the association will improve matters considerably.

In the car, keep your body language calm and do not keep petting your dog in anticipation of it developing a fear. Dogs are good at exploiting humans in the cuddles department by pretending to be frightened.

Let one person get your puppy used to travelling in the car. My wife is softer than I am: I would ask her to do it.

If nausea accompanies your dog's anxiety then a visit to your vet is needed.

'Anxiety' and 'fear' are generally used as interchangeable words. Anxiety means the dog is worried that something bad might happen whereas fear means something bad has happened.

Look at the recent history of your training and try to spot if a fearful moment has caused concern in your dog's mind.

Train Each Dog Separately

Sometimes dogs run away and stay away for hours. One minute they are there and the next minute they are gone. They have simply vanished.

This happens most often when the owner is walking two or more dogs. Once the habit becomes embedded it is almost impossible to break.

I can remember training two puppies that were brothers. One was dominant and far less tender and sensitive than the other. Each needed a different approach to training but I made the mistake of believing that I could train both at the same time.

The result was that when I shouted a command to the dominant dog, I frightened the life out of the tender one and it ran away. It took me too long to work out what had happened and, by the time I did, the habit was well established in the tender dog. The result was that he made a career of running away because, whether I shouted or not, his anxiety made him believe that I was about to.

Look carefully at your dog and find out quickly what its level of anxiety is and don't cross the line. If you have two dogs, train each one individually. Two cannot be trained at the same time.

Chapter Twelve

A Wolf in Dog's Clothing

I have read quite a few books on the ancestry of the dog. None agrees on when it chose to live with man. None agrees either about when the dog, as we would recognise it, emerged.

However, almost all agree on its background: it developed from the wolf, the jackal and the fox, all of which evolved from a creature named *Miacis* that existed in the Eocene period.

Canis familiaris – the dog – has been man's partner for at least a million years. Selective breeding has been practised for just ten thousand.

It is reasonable to suppose that the dog started its long association with man as a hunter. When man settled on the land to farm it, dogs were reared to perform other tasks, such as herding and guarding. No change for man or dog has ever been complete or speedy, so the evolution of the partnership must have been very gradual.

If you watch a brace of sheepdogs working you will notice that hunting and herding involve the same movements and skills, except there is no kill. Much of the communication is dog to dog rather than man to dog.

I have studied wolves and can see enough in their behaviour to link them to the modern dog: their body language is almost identical, and breeds like the German Shepherd, the Chow Chow and the Husky certainly look similar to them.

R.I. Pocock, writing in 1935, suggested that four types of wolf contained the genetic information needed to develop all modern breeds of dog. That the modern dog can produce fertile offspring when mated to a wolf adds weight to the belief that we need to look no further for its ancestor.

The four types cited by Pocock are the Northern Grey Wolf, the Pale-footed Asian Wolf, the small Desert Wolf of Arabia and the Woolly-coated Wolf of Tibet and northern India.

Later research has tended to confirm this view and to throw doubt on work that seeks to involve other ancestors.

When wolves are hunting they communicate by body language and sound. As wearing down a prey animal can involve a chase of up to sixty kilometres, the wolves in a pack will often become separated. The howling sound they make is thought to be a way of indicating location to each other. Interestingly, when hunting, wolves run in single file almost as if they are cutting down the effort of passing through deep snow. It is only on curves that they separate. Observers have been able to count the number in a particular pack only by studying the footprints on a bend or curve.

In Israel twelve-thousand-year-old fossilised remains were found of a man and a dog. The man's hand lay on the dog's head and they were positioned side by side.

I would love to know how our partnership with dogs began. There must be a wonderful story of the first encounter between the two animals that have been best friends for so long. We can speculate, of course.

Both wolves and men survived through hunting. Perhaps the wolves picked at what was left of the animal man had killed, which led to them growing accustomed to each other and eventually hunting together.

Dog and Fox Speak

I can remember my first Border Collie, Annie, carrying on some sort of howling and barking conversation with mating foxes as we returned from the fields late one evening.

As it was winter, the fox making the sound might easily have been a cub issuing an abandonment or loneliness call. As Annie was just starting her season, I must favour the latter as a possibility.

They 'spoke' to each other for at least a quarter of an hour, taking it in turn to howl. Clearly it was neither random nor pointless, but it was certainly eerie. Gradually, the calls of the fox came closer and I suspect that if I had not been there a meeting would have taken place.

At the time I wondered how they could communicate with one another, and it is this inheritance of language, and the links between wild dogs, jackals, foxes, wolves and the domestic dog, that absorbs me rather than distant dates in history. If a dog can talk to a fox then the language has not changed.

Foxes and wolves have a global distribution so both might easily be ancestors of the domestic dog.

The Fox is Crafty

Many experts believe that the fox's much-vaunted intelligence has been exaggerated and that it is not as bright as legend supposes it. I am less sure than they are. There were stories in the West Country where I worked (and where foxes abound) of the animal's guile and intelligence.

One involved a fox that was infested with fleas. It picked up a stick in its mouth, then lowered itself into a pond or a stream and gradually submerged itself until the fleas, having nowhere else to go, ran up its body and head until they were all on the stick, which the fox then discarded. That seems like an awful lot of storytelling effort for something that wasn't true!

There are stories of the fox eluding the hunt by sitting on a gravestone in the churchyard where no hunt would dare to go: fact or pure fiction?

I have seen a fox totally outwit the hunt, sending humans, horses and hounds the wrong way. It ran across a field, jumped on to a length of compacted hedge, ran along the top for fifty yards or so, then turned and ran back the way it had come but making use of a gully, or fold, in the land.

From our bedroom window I watched the hounds streaming down towards the hedge while the fox ran in the opposite direction no more than fifty yards away from them.

Personally, I would not rush to disprove stories of the fox's cleverness.

The fox's tail is much longer than that of most dogs. When it runs across snow the tail brushes away the evidence of its passage. This, too, is cited by country folk as a sign of its cleverness, although it has more to do with the animal's anatomical design than intelligence.

A wealth of myth and legend surrounds Brer Fox.

A Team Animal

It interests me that the dog's ancestors share many of its characteristics. All of them lived in families, all worked as a team and all, like man, shared their skills to maximise their hunting success.

Neither man nor the ancestor of the dog was a sprinter that could run faster than its prey; both succeeded because they could run further than their quarry and because they could communicate with each other.

In the wild, females are usually the alpha animals and lead the hunt as well as organising the pack.

Marking Territory

Males mark the boundaries of the pack's domain so that all its members know where their territory ends and the next begins. Such marking enables different packs to avoid conflict.

The domestic dog behaves in exactly the same way, which is why your male dog spends so much time marking the same signposts every day.

It is also why a male dog is prone to mark territory that belongs to another dog, be it outdoors or in someone else's house – to his owner's extreme embarrassment.

If I brought one of my outside kennel dogs into the established territory of the two dogs that live in the kitchen it would reward me by marking immediately. This is a declaration of ownership – or, at least, of belonging. Even though the dog in question would know that it must not do such a thing indoors, the age-old urge to mark territory would overcome its training.

If the same dog lived in the kitchen it would not do it because there would be sufficient evidence of its tenure in its own doggy smells.

When a dog has an accident on a carpet any other dog is likely to re-mark the same spot. They are simply doing what comes naturally. If the smell is removed by cleaning, it is less likely to happen again.

When I take a group of mixed-sex dogs into a field the males make for the boundaries and mark all of their signposts again. The females are much more prone to scavenge. If a dead and rotting pheasant is to be found, it will be a bitch that discovers it. I always worry about dogs finding a carcass because the bones that are left can be dangerous if splintered.

The Ears of the Pack

One of my bitches has amazing hearing, but she can't run very fast; the other females use her as a finder. The instant she hears a rodent rustling in the long grass, she assumes a particular pose, a kind of freeze. Her ears are cocked, her eyes pinned intently on the area. All of the other bitches gallop to the scene to provide a working team. Though the signal is visual and the others might be looking in a different direction, there is never a delay in their response.

That is a specific communication, no noise, just pure body language, yet something else is happening too. Watch a bitch with her puppies and you will see exactly the same body language in wild dogs, wolves and foxes – greeting, begging and submission.

All of the body-language postures are echoed in the wild dog. It is in the observation of these signs that dog whispering finds its source and inspiration.

Foxes will dance in the snow, stabbing their front legs to dislodge a hidden mouse so that it breaks cover. My own dogs do exactly the same thing when they hear and smell a mole just beneath the surface of the ground.

When wild dogs hunt they pick out an animal that is either old or young, or one that is not as fleet as the rest of the herd.

What degree of reasoning is involved in that decision and how do they agree on the choice? Does the alpha animal make the decision and the others trust it?

Is it a Calculating Intelligence?

I don't know. I have observed the intelligence of one of my dogs gathering sheep so that I can check for a fly infestation, which will lead to maggots.

Misty has made a shortcut of her own: instead of bringing in all of the sheep she will select those with fly and leave the rest to browse in peace. Furthermore she makes the decision at amazing speed. In the time it takes me to climb the gate, the infected sheep are already in a pen that is at least two hundred yards away from me.

The first couple of times this happened I made her gather all the sheep, once we had treated those that needed it, to check her accuracy. There was no need. She had got it exactly right.

- How did she know which animals were infected?

- How did she know that they were the ones I wanted?

- How did she know that I wanted them in that particular pen?

The domestic dog has inherited more than the language from its ancestors.

In a sheepdog trial, at the point of 'shedding' the sheep – separating the one with a brightly coloured collar – I lost my nerve. Bob saw what had happened and carried out a perfect six-move sequence, not only separating the one with the collar but holding it ten yards or so from the others.

The really clever part of his action followed. Once a successful shed has been completed to the judges' satisfaction, they blow a horn. I watched Bob's ears stand up to listen. The moment he heard the horn he returned the sheep to its proper place.

If you watch wild dogs you will see how a family works together to achieve its end. The domestic dog is the same, but it has a different family. You.

So, when someone asks you about your dog's pedigree, answer, '*Canis familiaris.*' It's a mighty good one!

Chapter Thirteen

Breeding Aggression

I remember with sadness a dog I was training; it was a working dog more suited to the hustle and bustle of the stockyard than being indoors. The owners had left it with two small children and it nipped one. They sent it immediately to the vet to be put down.

When I heard about it I asked if I could have the dog in the event that I could get to the vet quickly enough to save it. I was too late by just a few minutes. Later I did a bit of detective work and discovered that the children had tied a rope round its neck.

I wondered how tight the rope had been – and how much patience the dog was expected to show in such a situation. One thing is certain: there will be just one loser in such a confrontation, whoever caused it. In any such situation the first casualty is justice.

How to Make a Nice Dog Nasty

Make a mental note that untrained children should not be in charge of a dog unless the dog and the children are trustworthy. This means outdoors every bit as it means in.

Children love to run, arms outstretched, hoping that pet dog will enjoy the game. The dog *will* enjoy it, but flapping arms and the excitement of a chase are an open invitation – a positive encouragement even – for it to bite. Torn shirts are evidence that this 'encouraging training' works well.

The bites might start with gentle mouthing but the situation is one that could not be better designed to cause a nip and it might well happen to someone other than the owner.

To then pass on the blame to the dog carries no justice and no honesty whatsoever.

The same observation goes for adults: do not play chase with your dog and most certainly do not wrestle with it. It might well seem like harmless fun at the time but the dog will not be able to distinguish between a frail old neighbour and a willing participant. To a dog, there is often a very thin line between pretend and real.

This sort of treatment is akin to saying to your dog, 'Chase anyone you like and jump up when you feel like it.' Worse, in fact, as it really amounts to a command to do it. Dogs take more from body language than any other sign, which is why dog whispering actually works.

It won't be much good explaining to the mother of a little child that the jump that flattened her beloved was just a friendly action.

Of course dogs like to play, but a harmless game of collect-the-ball will enhance your training rather than destroy it.

Do not encourage your dog to jump up to receive its cuddle

because it might not instantly tell the difference between your best suit and your dog-walking clothes; neither will it discern the difference between fresh, clean spring grass and the most disgusting mud.

I have sat in kitchens talking to young parents while their child pulled the dog around mercilessly. Not once did they tell the child off but if the dog got too rough it was in immediate trouble.

This kind of treatment will quickly ruin the dog's good nature and eventually it will pay the price.

If you have difficulty in appreciating what I am saying here then you could well be the wrong sort of person to own a dog. Better, though, that I offend you than let a dog pay the ultimate price.

The more I read about aggression in dogs, the more I realise that it is not an easy behavioural problem to deal with. It comes in many forms and has many causes. Let's go back to the beginning. The dog comes from the wolf or, perhaps more accurately, all evidence points to the wolf as one of its ancestors.

Aggression is part of the wolf's makeup.

In fact, aggression is a vital self-survival component that enables it to flourish in the wild. The wolf tribe, or pack, has many mechanisms to avoid aggression becoming dangerous within the pack.

The alpha wolf dominates and the others learn to show signs of submission which circumnavigate actual damaging conflict. It would not benefit a wolf pack to have injured members incapable of hunting.

Still a Wolf at Heart

The domestic dog has not entirely lost the wolf's influence in its background, and aggression is part of its inheritance. Aggression is normal in the domestic dog. Male dogs are as well versed in aggressive and submissive posturing as their ancestors were, and still are.

If you watch male dogs they perform a kind of ritual that is far more about posing than action. It is designed that way so that dominance and submission can be achieved by body language rather than fighting.

The trouble comes when the wolf/dog does not live with its tribe any more but with a new family called humans.

In this new 'pack' there might be a large alpha animal, a slightly smaller one and perhaps two little ones. None of them speaks with the signs that a wolf or dog pack uses. What is my status in this pack? it wonders.

If the children run, encouraging the dog to jump up, then it reasons that they are cubs or puppies that want to play. In puppy play, bites are acceptable; in play with children, they most definitely are not.

Imagine that the larger alpha animal is away and the puppy has grown to sexual maturity. It sees itself, perhaps, as number two in the pack hierarchy – might it now put up some resistance to its rival?

Excessive barking and a reluctance to obey could be the manifestation of the dog's belief.

Violence Begets Violence

If the alpha human beats the dog and takes no notice of its signs of submission then the dog thinks that the pack's currency is violence; so violence, which is good enough for the pack leader, is good enough for the dog. The dog might not respond to the alpha human's treatment but might think it acceptable to bite a smaller, weaker pack member.

Before this tale gets too grim I ought to state that, with fifteen dogs altogether, I experience no violent or dangerous moments between human and dog.

Peaceful coexistence is easy to achieve.

When one dog meets another in an open space they have the advantage of each understanding the other's body language but, unlike the intimacy of the wolf pack, they might well be strangers, not knowing their own status or that of the dog facing them.

Imagine that you have been put into a totally alien culture, not knowing the language or the ways. Then you can begin to understand the difficulties the dog faces in a human environment.

Dogs are actually civilised but in their own 'culture' rather than in ours. I notice that my alpha dog is ageing fast and is losing the physical and mental edge that elevated him to that position. All of my other dogs act like carers, treating him with respect and consideration. A couple of the other males know they could easily displace him but decline to do so, unless he is not actually with them, when they assume the control that was his. Humans rarely achieve that sort of respect and consideration.

What are the Causes of Aggression?

Aggression is unintentionally caused by the ignorance of the owner.

Physical punishment is likely to increase aggression. Men react more strongly than women to disobedience, and are much more likely to see domination as a cure.

The 'I am tougher than you' attitude will actually cause aggression in a dog and will achieve the opposite of the intention.

Violence begets violence!

Data from German owners of dogs involved in dogfights showed that the dog that initiated the fight was most commonly owned by a male with a comparably high education and income. A high proportion of this group felt that training a dog was not necessary.

I believe that there are three main reasons for aggressive behaviour in dogs:

- Lack of understanding by a dog's owners

- Overbreeding in a search for perfect appearance or functional excellence

- Removing a puppy too early from the 'educating' influence of its mother

If you look carefully you will see that each of the reasons cited amounts to a lack of understanding.

In the show-dog world a disproportionate amount of effort is put into the acceptable appearance of a dog: it has to conform to the standards of the breed. I wonder whether perhaps less care is taken with the nature and temperament of the dog in the rush to achieve cosmetic excellence . . .

An interesting snippet. When Poodle puppies were housed and raised with wolf cubs, the juvenile wolves showed increasing numbers of appeasement behaviours and submitted to the Poodles. The young Poodles, on the other hand, engaged in increasing numbers of aggressive behaviours towards the young wolves.

Breeding dogs, like my own Border Collies, for a specific purpose – in this case herding – is a way to potentially increase the tendency towards aggression: the breeder might well neglect temperament in favour of greater herding skills.

Both the show breeder and the task breeder may have put their ambition ahead of the dog's needs, in the search for what they would describe as a better dog. (A prospective buyer should take this into consideration.)

If the person selling the puppy goes on and on about its magnificent 'show' looks or its wonderful working ability but says nothing about its good nature, the buyer might just be in the company of a fanatic too driven by achieving show or working excellence to see the importance of the dog having a nice temperament.

Taking a puppy away from its mother and siblings before the lessons of life have been learned is to my mind one of the great causes of aggression.

Aggression can also be shown to another dog whether it is a stranger or familiar. If the less dominant dog displays submissive behaviour then the fight will not develop but consist merely of posturing.

Sometimes when dogs live with each other, dominance has already been established and the confrontation will be confined to the odd mutter or growl.

Aggression between dogs that are strangers does happen (most often between males) but though the observation is easy to make, a remedy is hard to find.

The causes of such aggression can't really be pinpointed without knowing the precise details of the encounter. Being realistic, you can at least try to make sure that your own dog is not aggressive, but you can do little about other people's dogs.

Maybe some of what I said earlier will provide a clue as to the sort of person who might own an aggressive dog. Pitiful though it is, the best advice I can give you is: look at the dog's owner as well as at the dog. If the owner is demonstrating a lack of control over the dog, then keep a wide berth.

There can be exceptional conditions that increase the likelihood of aggression both to humans and other dogs. Years ago I went to a farm to collect some eggs. It was my habit to go on the same day each week. On that occasion, there had just been a fierce thunderstorm, complete with spectacular lightning. The air was close and oppressive.

I got out of my car just as the farmhouse door opened and I saw a large Old English Sheepdog running straight at me. When it reached me it knocked me flat on my back, then bit my shoulder and my arm.

I had a Newfoundland and a Labrador in the back of my car but they were quiet so I don't think they had contributed anything to what happened.

I am sure that under normal circumstances the Old English would have reacted quite differently but because of the abnormal weather and its fear of the crashes and bangs of the storm, the dog behaved in a way that its owner could not predict. It may even have believed that I had something to do with the storm.

On another occasion, after a show at a school, a child rushed straight through the middle of my pack of dogs to talk to me. I was standing next to my truck, which is the dogs' 'mobile home'. Seen from the dogs' point of view, this could be read as a double, all-out attack – one on me and another on their territory. The result was that the second in line in the hierarchy of my pack knocked the child down.

I did all of the apologising, as though total blame was mine, but in truth there was blame on both sides. I failed to realise how the dogs might interpret a friendly action as an aggressive one. The parents were not looking out for their child.

I think that all we can do to avoid such incidents is to be as aware as we possibly can be not only of the dangers we can see but also of the interpretation a dog might make.

Chapter Fourteen

Behavioural Problems

What is a behavioural problem?

My own definition would be a deep-seated, or embedded, form of abnormal behaviour.

It could also be described as an amplified, exaggerated or excessive use of the normal patterns of canine behaviour.

To give you an example: one would expect a dog to be fearful when there is a reason to be so, but to be fearful all the time is abnormal.

Continual barking is not something that a dog is born with but something that is caused.

I do not believe that dogs are born with psychological problems but that problems are brought about by the treatment they receive. I am not qualified to say 'never'.

Mother Knows Best

I think that many problems are caused by removing a puppy from its mother before it is twelve weeks old. Mother doesn't just feed her puppies, she educates them in the ways of the dog.

All wild animals teach their offspring how to survive and the domestic dog is no different. When to submit to a senior or stronger dog in order to avoid a damaging conflict is but one example.

In a litter, puppies play-fight for a great deal of the time. Though their teeth are sharp and can inflict pain they do little damage to each other, but the process teaches them that to show submission by body language avoids serious consequences.

This lesson will be invaluable in later life.

I suspect that aggression, either towards other dogs or towards humans, can be brought about in a dog that did not learn the lessons of play-fighting with the other puppies in its litter because it was taken away from their company too soon.

To put it plainly, if a puppy is removed from its mother too soon, it is deprived of the necessary teaching that will equip it to live a life of normality, and this premature removal from mother's influence will make the puppy much more prone to some form of insecurity.

An old farmer friend described it thus:
'A puppy removed from its mother too early
will think it is a human.'

As it is not a human, but a dog, it will not flourish if it receives human influence before it has had time to learn how to be a dog. It is more likely to try dominance techniques with lesser members of its human family because it did not have time to learn the language of coexistence with its dog family.

A good breeder should know this and appreciate that the puppy's welfare will be much improved if it has time to learn all that its mother can teach it.

When we describe our dog as a Labrador or a Red Setter we forget that this is only a title that we have given a particular type of dog.

The dog itself has no idea what it is, even if its genes guide it eventually to be a Red Setter. So, a working dog doesn't know how to be a working dog until we put the opportunity in its way and help it through teaching. And no dog will know where it stands in the hierarchy unless we have the wisdom to realise that its mother is the only one that can teach it and to give her the time to do this by leaving the puppy with her for at least twelve weeks.

Whatever the breeder says, insist on not collecting your puppy until it has had time to learn. Problems galore can develop with a puppy taken from mother before nature's time. Nature's time is when weaning is totally completed and this will be indicated by the mother's unwillingness to feed her puppy any more.

A Lack of Understanding

Imagine the impact of the following scenario and the long-lasting damage it could do. You purchase a puppy and take it home before its mother has had time to teach it and before it is ready to leave her.

It is not used to feeding itself with solids and still partly depends on its mother's milk.

It is taken away from her and driven in a car to a new place.

(A fearful experience creating an association that does not bode well.)

In fear, it wets the floor and immediately gets told off.

How many problems have been kicked into being by a lack of understanding?

- It still needs its mother and will try to replace the lost one with you. What do you know about being a puppy or about being a puppy's mother?

- It does not know how to eat solids properly.

- It is suddenly in a car and the new experience is compounded by the unhappy association with leaving its mother too early. This could easily result in it being a bad traveller.

- It is thrust into a new and strange environment and wets the floor in response. It then gets told off. Mother would not have chastised it but simply cleaned up after it. Result: fear and confusion.

- Then at night it is left all on its own in an unfamiliar place. It cries and gets told off all over again. Mother would have pulled it within her comfort until it went to sleep peacefully. Result: fear, confusion and mistrust.

Not exactly the ideal way to start a new life, is it? If a puppy starts badly the scars will last for life and could well be manifested in some sort of behavioural problem.

Wait until the puppy is old enough and better equipped to adjust to this hugely traumatic change in its life.

Looking after and training a dog properly is much more rocket science than you might have imagined.

Molly, who I have mentioned before, stayed with her mother for at least two months longer than the recommended twelve weeks and, as a result, had actually learned about many things before she came to me.

Good and Bad Habits

Don't be tempted to extend that line of argument, though. When it comes to working, a dog will learn bad habits from its mother as well as good ones. If the mother bites and the puppy sees her do so, then it will bite too.

When I train my pups I enlist the help of the older, wiser dogs but no single dog will help with every manoeuvre because no one dog can do every move properly. Each has an outstanding virtue and its help will only be sought in the area at which it excels. My intention is that the puppy will learn from the near-perfect example it has seen and end up better at all of the manoeuvres.

I can remember an old farmer saying things like, 'My first dog was not much good and none have been since.' What had happened was entirely the farmer's fault. He hadn't trained the first, but the first trained the second, so all the bad habits were simply passed on.

Where I lived there were shepherds who had a succession of good dogs and this was mainly because they had trained the first one well.

Damage is caused by taking a puppy away from its mum too

soon; it is also caused by the treatment the dog receives as it starts to grow up. Ignorance and misunderstanding are the root of most of the problems that can eventually result in abnormal behaviour.

The physical mistreatment of a dog, as a form of punishment, will turn it into either a fearful or an aggressive one. If the language it understands is physical violence, then physical violence is what it will deliver.

If you try to understand the young dog and treat it accordingly as it gets older it will care about understanding you and the result will be one of real harmony.

I have said earlier that dog whispering is holistic and that empathy must be present in all that you do with your dog.

Perhaps the clearest way to emphasise this is to put it another way: treat your dog the way you would like to be treated or, at least, try to put yourself in its place.

My vet kindly lent me a copy of the BSAVA *Manual of Canine and Feline Behavioural Medicine*. In this excellent book the following behavioural problems are listed and dealt with from a veterinary perspective, along with many other behavioural abnormalities.

Only the main headings have been included. I think the ones shown here are the most useful to the domestic dog owner:

- Aggression

- Anxiety

- Attention-seeking

- Barking

- Car Travel

- Chewing and Other Destructive Behaviour

- Fear

- Fighting

- Punishment

- Soiling

The dog-whispering techniques that I have recommended (along with thoughtful nurture) will prevent all of these problems.

I have owned twenty-five dogs and hundreds of others (of all sorts of different breeds) have passed through my hands in my training capacity and only three have had what I would call serious problems.

All three were rescue dogs that showed signs of mistreatment by previous owners. If you own a dog from its puppy stage onwards then following what I have said will prevent problems occurring.

If you take on a rescue dog there is no guarantee. Whatever the previous owner did will have affected its behaviour.

However, there is no more rewarding experience than resettling a dog and giving it a comfortable home and a good life. There are many rescue dogs out there, not through any fault of their own but either because of misfortune or because they were chosen by the wrong owner.

Chapter Fifteen

The Best Glue is Love

Though they take time to make their choice, most dogs arrive at a human favourite. I often hear couples say, 'It's her dog, or his: I can't do a thing with it.' Loosely interpreted, this means that the person who 'can't do a thing with it' doesn't really want to and something has alerted the dog to this. Maybe it is the level of attention and affection the dog receives that tells it which pack member it should attach itself to. The dog has made the right choice!

Sometimes it is a different kind of bonding in which the dog prefers one person to train it but sits close to the other in the evening and makes a fuss of them.

In a balance sense, this must be the ideal. Sometimes, the dog will do what the trainer asks but does it remotely so that the trainer always feels that the dog's mind, attentions and affections are elsewhere. It isn't wholeheartedly with them – like a Welsh dog I worked at a training school. To be fair to the dog, it wasn't mine, so there was no reason why it should show me any affection. It did everything I asked of it more competently than most dogs would, but it was a cold-blooded, remote-controlled, robot-like experience. I could not read its intentions and I'm sure it could not feel mine.

There is a need for rapport between human and dog.

In rare cases a dog likes someone outside the family better than anybody else. A lady I know works for people who have a dog that obviously loves her and enjoys nothing more than coming home with her for an evening beside the fire.

Dogs will give affection and pay attention but it has to be given to them first. Sometimes, I suspect, one person in the family really wants the dog and the others tolerate it.

I have had a couple of dogs, over the years, that never quite felt like mine. As a shepherd, out working with a dog all day, I knew it was important that the dog identified totally with me otherwise neither of us would ever work well in what is a close partnership. What I mean is that any one of my own dogs would be reading me. If I told them to go right but the real answer was left my own dogs would pick the correct direction, knowing that they have that kind of licence with me.

I have observed that there appear to be three ways to a dog's heart:

- Exercise

- Food

- Kindness

Which order they come in is highly debatable.

Bonding

There are several simple ways to get your dog to bond with you. You need to give it plenty of your time. You also need to be the one who feeds and grooms it. Most of all, you must make sure that the training process is always calm and that irritability never creeps in.

You will not have to do this for the whole of your dog's life but certainly during the impressionable puppy period (though you will always have to be generous with your time). The aim is not to have the dog stuck permanently to your heels, or to persuade it that you are nicer and more worthy of its attention than your partner, but simply to build a foundation for the most effective training.

The training has to be wholeheartedly enjoyed,
both by dog and human.

If a dog is not bonding with me, to the extent that we are not making the kind of progress I would want, I use a ploy that always seems to work. Not only does it work but the beneficial results are almost immediate – and, in most cases, *absolutely immediate*!

The Away Day

Most of my dog demonstrations are at country fairs, held over a weekend, usually about ninety minutes' drive from my home.

I hitch up the caravan and pack two tasty meals, one for the unresponsive dog and one for me. The travel is as leisurely as I can make it. When we arrive, apart from getting the caravan ready for the weekend, the whole of the time is spent walking, without a lead, and there is no training at all.

At mealtimes we eat our food at the same time, not with me sitting at the table and friend dog on the floor but both together on the grass. With one particular dog that was slow to respond, I went even further: I made sure that we ate the same food off the same plate. It was not dog food but bread, butter and sausages. I would give him a piece, then break off another piece for myself.

You would think this might encourage the dog to scrounge when it gets back home but, strangely, it does not. The dog is able to see this as a different and exceptional happening. I very often shared a Cornish pasty with my working dogs when we were miles away from the farmhouse and they never expected the same treatment at home.

In between times are spent sitting comfortably, watching TV, with both of us on the same seat. Invariably the dog moves up to sit as close as it can.

After a slow day we drive home.

No bad habits have been started, because dogs know the difference between a caravan bench seat and the sofa back home, but we have bonded.

It has always worked and I have always noticed a huge and lasting difference in our relationship and especially in the attitude of my dog when training starts again.

Maybe you can't do the same thing but you could get very close to it using just your car. This 'away day', where all your attention is focused on the dog, changes things beyond belief.

I have never been in doubt about a dog's loyalty and affection after returning from one of these bonding sessions.

The dogs I've done this with have been the timid type that needed reassurance. It is surprising, knowing this, that just one day could have such a dramatic outcome.

Gentle is Best

I am not absolutely sure about the validity of this next statement but I do believe that the reason for a dog's timidity is not so much a result of its genes (though these may have contributed) but more to do with something I did wrong in its early training.

Maybe during lead training I was just a little too harsh. With some dogs even a short spell of irritability can really damage any chance of progress being made. After all, if I was irritable once surely I will be again.

I do not think that there is anything to choose between men and women as trainers. I have seen harsh women as well as men. One thing is absolutely for sure, though: being overly hard with a dog will take the process backwards not forwards.

I think that some men will have problems if they try to rely on the macho need for dominance, especially those who own tough dogs. Even dogs that have a heritage of being bred to fight will respond to kind and gentle training.

I well remember the ridicule I attracted when I started with the dog-whispering method. It stopped as soon as my dogs began to outperform those of my detractors.

I can also recall a farmer's wife working with a little bitch that the farmer had trained but could do nothing with. She produced a sublime display of complicated sheep herding because her approach was about being gentle rather than domineering.

Dog training consists of things you know and things you have a hunch about. Following a strong hunch often leads to dramatic improvement.

The hunch is not about how you do a particular thing, but why your dog does not want to do it.

If you make a real effort to understand what is going on in your dog's mind and respond with empathy, the result will be better than you could ever have imagined.

If you are faced by the problem of a dog that is reluctant when it comes to being trained, it will profit you both greatly if you pay serious attention to a better bonding.

Chapter Sixteen

Tailor the Training

As I drive to the set-aside field that a farmer friend so kindly lent me for training purposes, I see several dogs. Some are very well trained.

An old man with a black Labrador either makes a sign or calls a command and instantly, wherever his dog is, it sits down, eyes attentively on him, and waits until I have – slowly – driven past. I notice that his dog never sets foot on the road but stays on the grass verge.

The owner must trust his dog implicitly. Whether that is enough I don't know. I would much prefer my dogs to sit beside me, just in case something unexpected happened. But this carping criticism is not really warranted because the dog does exactly, and instantly, what its owner tells it to do. That is a well-trained dog.

Another lady calls her two dogs when she sees me coming. They run right up to her, tuck themselves tightly against her legs and then sit. That is not just good training but perfection!

One rather overweight dog, always minus an owner, snaps

at the wheels of my car as I pass. Obviously, its owner's idea of exercise is to open the door and let it out. The dog's end can be prophesied.

The first two owners might just read this book; the last one won't.

Professional Resistance

When I worked at my first theme park the owner thought it would be a good idea to send me to a Welsh training centre to gain an advanced certificate in dog handling. He suggested that once I had passed, I could train the other dog demonstrators in the correct way to do things. I took copious notes and made diagrammatic sketches of everything I was taught. When I tried to pass on the information to the other demonstrators they just didn't want to know. I wondered how their dogs would ever learn when they were shackled to an owner who thought they knew it all.

The training was specific to working sheepdogs. It was superb and included much that was suitable for obedience training. I trained my first dog, Annie, far beyond competence because I had noticed that the training acted as wonderful therapy for a nervous dog. As she was my first Border Collie and I was not looking to work her professionally (though I later did), I taught her general obedience first, then went on to teach her to run to the left, the right, lie down, get up, etc.

Once the first stage was complete I added all sorts of sophistications, such as running round a distant tree, first to the right, then to the left. I also taught her to count at a distance – which means to walk however many paces I asked for.

When we moved to Devon she started to work sheep, even though she had never seen them before, because she had learned all of the necessary moves in her basic training and because I had taken the trouble to read up on her breed.

All of the lessons in this book were included in her training. She took one year to complete them.

Different Dogs

Dogs vary, of course. Some learn very quickly, others are slower. Gun dogs, like Springer and Cocker Spaniels, will learn quickly, especially the distance training.

Springers are hyper so might prove more difficult to train when it comes to the real close-up work but they are as bright as buttons and more than capable of learning.

Cocker Spaniels are neat and precise and quick learners, good close up and far away.

Many dogs prefer the close-up training. If you can read a book about the breed you have it might well give you some hints that will prove useful in the training. The different breeds don't just look different, they vary in terms of behaviour patterns too: underneath, though, they are still descended from the wolf.

I am sure you will understand that there isn't room in this book to deal individually with each of the two hundred or so breeds that exist today, but the dog-whispering system of training will work for all.

A Dummy for a Gun Dog

What this means is that Spaniels, Labradors and Retrievers will learn quicker if you include some sort of retrieving element in their training. Gun-dog trainers use a 'dummy' – a mouth-sized kind of stuffed canvas bag. When it is thrown, the dog learns to bring it back and release it into the trainer's hand or drop it at his feet. Because gun dogs have been bred for generations to do this they find the exercise both natural and exciting.

Giving your dog something that it was bred to do will speed up the training considerably as well as making it much more fun. Hiding the dummy under a bush or in long grass, then encouraging your dog to find it, will provide a lot of enjoyment for both dog and you.

Collies like nothing better than circling. If there are two or three of you out walking, the Collie will try to herd you together.

Teaching your Collie to run right and left will exercise it and keep it mentally stimulated. This can be fairly easily done by using hand signals or throwing a ball to the right (or left) with the appropriate call.

For training purposes a dummy is even better than a ball and is great for teaching any breed of dog to run right or left. All you have to do is to throw the dummy to the right or left while calling the command. Of course, you will have to repeat the manoeuvre many times.

A dummy is also a great aid for teaching a dog to 'drop' on command – especially relevant for dogs who make a pastime out of picking up every unacceptable thing they come across. Throwing the dummy will discourage them from picking up other things and will prove an absolute delight for the stick-loving dog – and is far less dangerous.

166

In Wales, at the turn of the last century, there was a blacksmith who was also a very successful sheepdog trialist.

According to legend, he would tie two pieces of string to his dog's collar, one on each side, and while he was working in the smithy, his sons would gently pull first the left string, then the right, issuing the correct command with each pull. Apparently he won a great many trials because his dog had such a wonderful grasp of left and right.

Out of interest, shepherds call 'come by' for a clockwise movement and 'away to me' for an anticlockwise movement. They are asking their dog to run a complete or partial circle in order to flank a flock of sheep. (Many pet dogs will show the history of their breeding by running round and round their owner, a tendency that becomes even more pronounced if there is a group of people out walking.) For our purposes, right and left will suffice.

Some larger dogs won't thank you for making them run excessively. Neither will Pugs, Bulldogs and the like, so keep their training based on shorter distances.

For small dogs, like the Sheltie, I would keep all training fairly close; if you look at the dog's physique you will see that it was not designed for hard running.

Breeders will tell you not to let your puppy jump excessively or run up and down stairs until it is older than six months, as the strain on less than fully developed joints might be too severe and cause damage.

If your dog rejoices in running like mad, give it plenty of opportunity to do so. If it wasn't built to be an athlete, don't try and turn it into one.

Afghans, Whippets, Greyhounds and Salukis will love you for letting them run.

I would not allow a puppy or an older dog to over-run; the puppy needs time to develop and the older dog won't have the necessary stamina. They will prefer the close-up work.

I can remember little Molly, who was the apple of my eye, running in a trial one warm day. By the time we got to the pen, which is the last test, we were miles in front of the opposition on points. I gave the command to move up but Molly just stayed down. I did not persist as I could see that all was not as it should be.

Later I took her to the vet, who listened carefully to her chest, then told me she had a heart murmur. So, before you run your dog around, do make sure that it is up to it. It is well worth taking your dog for a check-up first.

The heart murmur did not last, by the way, and Molly controlled our pack right up to the day of her death. I can't help noticing that none of our other dogs will sit in her resting position in the house even though she has been gone for two years now.

Mongrels are every bit as good at the learning process so don't worry if you don't know what your dog's original breed was.

Remember, though, to apply the athletic/non-athletic appearance test before running it hard. My very first dog was a mongrel and even as an eight-year-old boy I found him to be highly intelligent and wonderfully responsive.

They are Much Brighter Than You Think

When I am watching obedience and agility competitions on TV, I am conscious of the fact that the dog is capable of doing far more than is being asked of it.

I am always puzzled when the owner runs round with the dog as it negotiates the various obstacles in an agility competition. I am puzzled because I have never seen a shepherd who thinks it necessary to run round the sheep with his dog.

The dog would be more than a bit miffed if he did.

Dogs That Dance

At lots of the shows I go to, there are ladies who demonstrate dancing with, usually, Border Collies. Each dog matches its handler's movements with absolute precision, and both handler and dog move in perfect time to the music.

As a purist who believes that Border Collies are made to work sheep, I found the first demonstration I watched not entirely to my taste. But the more I watched, the more I appreciated it. The dog is challenged mentally as well as getting a whole lot of good exercise, and, most importantly, it is happy and fulfilled.

It is very skilful on the part of both the dog and the handler and really does demonstrate just how tuned in to each other they are.

If the ladies who dance with dogs need to practise a part of their performance that is less than perfect, they don't have to go through their whole routine each time. It isn't the music that the dogs take their cue from but the movement of a particular segment, which they then practise over and over.

The same discipline applies to the training you are giving to your dog.

Keep it Up

Each day include just one or two of the sessions to keep your dog sharp and to maintain the attention it will have enjoyed in training. It would be unkind to stop suddenly, like going from real excitement to deadly boring in one go.

The reason that dogs enjoy training is because it provides mental and physical exercise and enhances bonding with you.

I know a very famous dog trainer who often appears on the same arena show schedule as me. The last time I saw her I asked if she was going to practise with her dogs before the show. Her answer was that the dogs knew exactly what they were doing so there was no need for practice.

I did not comment at the time but did think to myself that human athletes know what they are doing but still practise like mad.

Two schools of thought: I believe that the more times a dog practises, the better its performance; and the more *you* practise, the better *you* get.

Chapter Seventeen

Dogs are What They Eat

The dietician's favourite line is, 'We are what we eat.' This is just as true for dogs. I often hear owners complaining that their dog is a fussy eater: 'He'll only eat the best chicken, you know.' If you offer a dog the best chicken, then that is what it will want.

Fussy eaters are most often created
by fussy feeders.

A vet presented with a behavioural eating problem would try to ascertain why you wanted a dog or what the dog represents to you. Is it a child substitute? Are you feeding it in order to sustain it or because you get satisfaction from spoiling it?

I have a very old-fashioned view about feeding. I would feed a puppy in a most generous fashion, especially if it has a lot of growing to do. A puppy is going to increase its size far quicker and more dramatically than a human baby will. It will go from a ball of fluff to a virtually full-grown dog in around nine months or so. It needs the fuel to build that growth, but it has to be the right fuel.

Puppies need higher levels of nutrients than older dogs, so proprietary brands contain an excess of nutrients over those needed by a mature dog. I like substantial puppies! They can be slimmed down easily enough once they start running but I don't like to see adult dogs whose backs resemble coffee tables.

There is food that is tailored to the dietary needs of older dogs. Of course we can always view the claims made by producers of dog food with a certain amount of scepticism, but the other side of the story is that commercial companies realise the value of developing specialist foods for the various stages in a dog's life. If the food is good and does what the manufacturer says it will, then pet owners will keep using it.

I have been sponsored for twelve years by Pascoes, of East Yorkshire, in return for the coverage that our dog shows generate, in terms of actual appearances and attendant publicity. I had been using their food long before they decided to sponsor me.

When I was running the North Devon Sheepdog Breeding and Training Centre we always had lots of puppies and it was important to me that we used a scientific, rather than rule-of-thumb, system of feeding. As our dogs also took part in food-testing trials for Pascoes it became obvious to me that scientifically tailored feeding showed huge benefits in terms of health, vitality and stamina. The test was thorough: two dogs were fed on the existing food and two on the new formula. We monitored the reaction of the dogs to both types and watched their energy levels during hard running.

You should start your puppy on soft food and feed it four or even five times a day. As it grows older reduce the frequency of the meals so that at six months it is down to two a day. Puppy food is usually dry, so soak it in hot water for an hour first, then feed when

DOGS ARE WHAT THEY EAT

soft. Mother dogs regurgitate food for their puppies, which makes it soft, hence my 'natural' recommendation.

A little drop of gravy will make it all the tastier.

From six months to a year, very slowly, by gradual reduction, turn one of the meals into a snack and build the other meal until eventually at, say, thirteen months the dog is eating just one main meal a day. My preference is for the main meal to be fed in the afternoon or evening as it gives the dog a whole night to digest it before exercise starts again the next day. I also think dogs sleep better on a full stomach.

Some dog trainers recommend two meals a day, but as the dog is a carnivore, rather than a herbivore, I believe that once a day is more in line with an eating habit that has evolved over millions of years. However, there may be some value in feeding an older dog twice a day.

It is best to avoid feeding your dog just before or just after exercise.

Do not indulge your dog by demand-feeding, or providing always-available food. When your dog has finished eating, pick up the bowl. I have noticed that dogs who have access to food at every hour of the day and night are far more likely to be poor or fussy feeders.

It stands to reason that if your dog is truly hungry, not only will it attack its food with far more gusto but it will also develop a routine in which it knows what to expect.

Fit as a Butcher's Dog?

I used to train a dog that belonged to a butcher. Each week I would turn up at his farm to find an even fatter creature than the week before.

It had all of the virtues of the working dog including the brainpower but, alas, its fat frame impeded its ability. It would never make a good active dog, and however much I told the butcher that the loss of a stone in weight would benefit his dog more than another hour of training, I don't think he ever heard me.

The butcher obviously believed that quantity was better than quality – though I suspect his dog had both.

*It isn't the amount you feed your dog but
the content that is all-important.*

I must admit that I am viewing feeding from the perspective of someone who wants a dog to work a long day and to have the energy to manage it without losing body weight. You should temper my recommendations with the advice your specialist breeder gives you. They will know the requirements of your dog's particular breed.

Kiwi shepherds I worked with at my first theme park fed their dogs six days a week instead of seven, but I would caution against that sort of deprivation, especially with a dog that is going to get through miles of hard running each day.

Snacks

A lot of people feed their dogs scraps in between meals. I have never met a dog that will say no to a fine piece of roast beef covered in tasty gravy, but bear in mind that we're talking here about a carnivore that in the wild would glut itself on meat from a kill, then not eat anything for two or three days.

Do give your dog scraps by all means, but mix them with its normal food and feed a regular amount according to a regular routine.

Pascoes advise:

Dogs should not be fed a set amount of food regardless of the energy content. A person would not normally eat the same weight of chocolate as they would mashed potatoes because the chocolate is higher in calories and would cause them to be overweight.

If the food is more concentrated in terms of calories they should eat less of it.

So, when you put the lovely Sunday dinner that Granny couldn't manage on the dog's plate, reduce the amount of its normal feed. A fat dog is not only going to be more prone to ailments but is destined to have a shorter life.

Overfeeding is to kill with kindness.

Let your head rule your heart when it comes to feeding.

When your dog gets older and exercises less, feeding should be adjusted to take this into account, and the type of food it needs should be looked at. Many manufacturers make food that is designed to meet the older dog's needs. Dogs eat to meet their energy demands.

If your dog goes off its food, do go and get it checked out by your vet. Often, loss of appetite is a sign of bad teeth or some other medical problem.

I would always favour natural foodstuffs over chemically enhanced varieties. Some tinned brands contain a cocktail of artificial additives and colorants and I find it hard to believe that these can be good for a dog's stomach. Such thoughts passed through my mind when I once saw the brightly coloured stain left on the pavement by a dog and wondered what it might have eaten. The stain stayed there for two or three days, even though it rained quite heavily.

A balanced diet has energy and essential nutrients in a correct ratio and acknowledges different requirements for different life stages – in other words, it is tailored.

Some diets claim to be suitable for dogs at all life stages. This cannot be accurate because puppies need a higher level of nutrients than adult dogs. If the food provides nutrients sufficient for a puppy it means excess nutrients for an older dog – or, worse, vice versa.

On the packet of dog food you buy there will be a feeding guide showing the recommended amount by breed and stage of life. It is worth remembering that dogs, like people, are individuals and that the energy required depends on resting metabolic rate, activity, growth, breeding and environment (temperature).

Nutritionists use feeding equations to work out how much food an individual animal needs but equations cannot be totally accurate.

The advice on the packet is a guide and no more than that. Apply common sense by monitoring your dog's body condition.

I have two unrelated bitches that eat more or less the same amount of food each day; one is stocky, the other slim. On the basis that their genes have governed their body shapes I shall keep their food as it is rather than fattening up the slim one and robbing the stocky one of its natural inheritance.

If you feed two dogs together and one gets fat while the other becomes skinny, there is probably some food-stealing going on. If this happens, it is best to feed the dogs in different rooms. Once the subservient dog becomes used to the other's stealing, it is likely to stop eating before the thief approaches and will lose even more of its dinner. This is especially true with one fast and one slow eater.

Dogs, like humans, can become anorexic. The best possible cure for this is a visit to your vet.

Just as we don't keep the wonderfully attractive physical shape we had when we were nineteen, dogs don't either. Ageing brings the same gravity challenges to dogs as it does to humans.

That does not mean you should allow your dog to develop a middle-age spread, or that you should adopt a starvation diet to keep it youthfully slim.

Pascoes again:

The golden rules of feeding are: feed once or twice each day. Small dogs, large, giant dogs and old dogs are better fed more frequently.

My golden rule would be to feed just once a day, but breeders of some small and giant dogs would just as strongly recommend twice (which is what I would do in the case of an old dog with a poor appetite). Whether one method is, scientifically speaking, better than the other, I cannot say. Much depends on what sort of food you choose and the application of a great deal of common sense.

When I worked on a farm my dogs used to eat meat and biscuits; the meals certainly looked attractive and tasty. I noticed, though, that on really heavy working days involving shearing or dipping, the dogs would run out of energy after a couple of hours (made up of bouts of work and resting). When we changed their food to a scientifically designed working-dog mixture their stamina improved beyond belief. The food in the bowl did not look as attractive but they ate it just as enthusiastically.

If you are going to change your dog's diet, do so by stages. Mix its normal food with the new food, then gradually reduce the old while increasing the new until just the new is being eaten. This way your dog will not notice the change and there is less chance of its digestion being upset.

Chapter Eighteen

Sorry, No History Available

My definition of a rescue dog is one that is rehomed. It might have come from a rescue centre or from 'a friend of a friend'. In the case of a breeder it may have been returned. Wherever it came from, the dog has suffered some kind of trauma.

Gem

Our Sheltie came to us because her owner had to go into a retirement home. Gem had been loved and well treated all her life, but even after a relatively smooth transition, the little dog still has major fears.

It does not take too much imagination to identify their source. First of all, the owner's husband had died. Then, after a few years, the old lady became frail and Gem lost her as well. Then Gem came into a house where there were dogs galore from a home where she was the only one. A huge and traumatic change.

The little dog now suffers real anxiety if one of us goes out, probably believing that, like her first owners, we will not be coming back.

Here is one doggy terror that cannot be made to go away. It might well be that all the resettling and erasing you try will not overcome your dog's insecurity, and compromises will have to be made. You might need to lower your expectations.

There is less chance of hitting near-perfection with a rescue dog than there is with one that has had a settled life. The work will be harder and much patience will be demanded of you.

But rescue dogs have one huge advantage. They are usually very affectionate once the resettling process has been completed.

Often the difficulty for the new owner is that there is no history available. I suspect that most rescue dogs are disposed of because the first owner was unable to cope and simply abdicated responsibility. There will of course be more reasons than I could shake a stick at.

If there is a history available, even if it is incomplete, try hard to note down as much as you can. It will prove invaluable.

Often a rescue dog is one that looked adorable as a puppy and was bought on the basis of a temporary infatuation, which did not last once the demanding realities of ownership became apparent.

Too often the new owner subconsciously carries an element of doubt with them, perhaps suspecting that it must have been some failing on the part of the dog. It is far more likely that the dog's problems were caused entirely by the first owner.

I have had four rescue dogs: three were returned as young dogs after being sold to the wrong owners; Annie was found on a busy road when she was around nine months old. I have also trained several other rescue dogs for their new owners.

Maybe guilt informed my actions more than objective thought with the ones who were returned with 'no good' labels attached. Any conscientious breeder who makes a real hash of owner choice will feel tremendously guilty because the mistake is costly for the dog. I worked out very carefully my method for stabilising the new relationship. I was determined not to make a second mistake.

With the returned dogs it was easier because I knew they would eventually recognise my voice. I knew that my voice would have stable and happy memories for the young dog. I also knew their breeding history and the characteristics of Mum and Dad inside out. It is much easier to see a particular trait and then be able to say, 'Oh yes, just like Dad.'

I set about establishing a dramatic contrast in their treatment based on a common-sense approach. I assumed that when they were newly sold puppies, their owners would have made an enormous amount of fuss of them but that this ardour probably started to cool once the dogs lost their fluffy, helpless, puppy appeal and became leggy and naughty.

My approach was not to make a huge puppy-type fuss of them – after all, they had seen that before and it had not lasted – but to offer them a calm and gentle stability that would perhaps make them think, 'It's not too bad here.' The cuddles would come later.

The fact that all of them (except Annie) were handed over from the back of a car gives a strong clue as to what went wrong with the relationship. It was one-way: the owner was unable, or perhaps unwilling, to put themselves in the dog's place. Their only concern was to get rid of the problem as fast as they could – no sensitivity, no consideration.

Picture the situation: the dog is about to experience a hugely traumatic moment; all it knows is about to be taken away. It is not allowed to get out of the car for a moment to meet and get to know the person it is shortly going to be living with, but is severely disadvantaged by being locked up in a confined area and then handed over, cold-bloodedly, transactionally, like a parcel.

I am always amazed when apparently reasonable, intelligent people behave so thoughtlessly and fail completely to realise how insensitive their actions are.

The dog is a sentient creature, giving love without restraint and with no strings attached. It takes only a moment to cause irreparable damage.

My recommendation to anyone taking on a rescue dog would be to think hard about how it must be for the animal. When I say 'think hard', I do not mean for a second or two but diligently over quite a period of time. The dog has probably enjoyed being loved to bits and then, with no inkling of what was to come, it was rejected.

How would you feel if it happened to you?

Try to ascertain what your dog's fears are and what it lacks.

That probably sounds hard to do, but careful observation will give you the answer to both. During this period, you will gain much knowledge about your dog, which will help to smooth the way. Just be as sensitive as you were when you made the decision to offer your dog a new home.

Contrary to what many people believe, a dog has a long memory. I still meet up with lots of dogs that I sold years ago and each one instantly recognises my voice. Given that they were twelve-week-old puppies when they left me, this is proof enough for me.

Try to think of your dog's new environment – your home – as a kind of hospital.

Allow a lengthy period of settling in before you even think about starting to train your new dog and don't begin until you can see that it is ready.

Concentrate on making its life as good as can be. But remember that it is a dog: don't cuddle it up in a duvet on the sofa or allow it to do anything that may become a habit that you will wish you hadn't encouraged.

There is no all-embracing rule or any kind of panacea for all ills, as each dog, its problems and its reaction to them, will differ enormously.

The Lost Dog

Annie, the dog I found on the road, was simply lost. We didn't just claim her as our own but tried hard to find out who her previous owner had been.

Later, her behaviour gave me some clues as to what might have happened to her. She was particularly frightened of noise, especially sudden noise. (Though, strangely, shotgun blasts and fireworks did not upset her at all.)

Once, when we were driving down the motorway to Devon, a lemonade bottle suddenly released some gas, making a loud fizzing sound. Annie leaped from the back of the car, over my wife's head, and landed neatly in her lap. Maureen was driving at the time, doing about 70mph, so it came as some surprise to find a dog sitting in her lap, staring into her eyes.

After we arrived in Devon, I once took Annie with me into a gents' toilet. The automatic flush dramatically did its job and the noise made Annie slip her collar and vanish in the direction of the main road. It took all of an hour to find her.

Though both of these events were not pleasant, at the time the information I gained from them proved useful. Once Annie had settled into her new life with us, I started pretty intensive training, figuring that what she needed was confidence. Because I was sympathetic to her problems, I carried it out with exaggerated kindness.

The rewards were great. Within a year she was working brilliantly and ended up as my star dog in demonstrations at theme parks. All of her fears had simply vanished.

Annie was the first dog I ever thoroughly trained but the method I used on her became the template for all of those that followed.

Interestingly, when Annie was around five years old I retrained her to work in Welsh at a much higher level than I had first managed. The second round of training was much harder for her and for me but she learned.

I have already mentioned that each of my dogs works to a different language so that each knows that I am speaking just to them. In the process of doing this I noticed that the older dogs had learned several languages. Bob, my lead dog, will work in any one of eight.

I pose an unanswerable question for myself and for you: if it is just the sound and the sound is different with each language, then how do they understand? I can only deduce that dogs are a lot cleverer than I would have estimated.

In the training of a rescue dog there is, I believe, some kind of magic button that can be pressed once located. If you can discover what the dog really needs and can supply it, the whole process will be made much easier.

Watching rather than doing could prove to be wise indeed.

Susie's 'Magic Button'

A little bitch called Susie came back to me because her owners found her just too energetic. I had made the classic mistake and not judged very well either her or the people that bought her. She was beginning to eat furniture for a pastime. This kind of behaviour suggests a bored dog. Both physical exercise and mental stimulation were missing from her life.

When I took her back, her terror suggested that she would never settle happily again.

That very afternoon three or four hundred sheep got mixed up with another flock at the theme park where we worked. They needed sorting out. All of my other dogs had been working hard in the hot sun and I didn't want to overtax them, so I took the newly arrived Susie. I hoped she would have some clue and figured we might just be able to manage because of the huge amount of energy she had at her disposal.

If I had stopped to think about it, I would have realised that it is impossible at a theme park to do anything privately and very quickly a huge crowd gathered by the side of the field to watch this much-vaunted shepherd neatly put things right. I was tempted to shout out that she had never done anything like this before and that she was untrained, but I resisted. Don't bad workmen always blame their tools? I need not have worried. Susie's year of bored frustration with owners that did not understand her needs was set right in a trice.

Three very smart moves from her, accompanied by a few meaningless whistles from me, and the sheep were back where they were meant to be. The crowd went home happy and so did little Susie.

Since that moment she has been joined to me by an invisible string. There was never any need to resettle her – no work, no effort.

So, look for the magic button. It might not be spotted as quickly as Susie's was but if you search hard you might well find it.

No Button Found

Prince, a rescue Newfoundland, came to me when I was too young and inexperienced. How I wish that there had been a book like this to help me get it right. I never found the magic button that would have put him back on course. Because Susie's magic button was found the day she came back to me, she settled immediately and just improved with each working day.

With a rescue dog I therefore recommend you take the following steps:

- Observe – look for the magic button

- Show consistent calmness

- Train as I have outlined in the earlier chapters

- Never, ever become impatient or irritable

The Older Rescue Dog

'Old' is a relative term. When it comes to training a dog I take old to mean around eight. The ageing process can be affected by so many things: breed, lifestyle, genes all play a part. If I were asked to define ageing I think I would say that it is an increasing inability to cope.

I have one dog who began to experience problems with his joints at around five years old. But ageing affects the mind as well as the body: it seems to be much more difficult for an older dog to take in the process of learning.

The best advice I can give is to take an older rescue dog to a good vet and have it checked over. The kennels it came from will probably not know its true age.

I would not subject a dog over seven years old to a training routine.

Chapter Nineteen

Dogs Need Routines

Imagine you are staying with rather eccentric friends. Sometimes they get up at seven, sometimes at midday. On certain days there might be breakfast, on other days none. To compound your difficulties, their pronouncements about the day's plans will be totally unreliable and everything is subject to change.

Their mood swings between happy and sociable or downright miserable. It wouldn't take long for you to decide to go home or, worse, to have the relationship break down completely.

This is how it is for a dog that is expected to live in a household with no routine – except that the poor dog cannot go home.

To make matters worse the dog is unable to voice its unhappiness and frustration. In time its lack of contentment will manifest in some behavioural problem.

I will say it yet again – dog whispering is holistic: your approach should be shaped by your dog's well-being in every aspect of its life. You can be sure that if something is not right in one department it will have a negative effect in others.

From observation I believe that dogs go through the same initial deductive process as us, but they cannot rationalise – or only to a much lesser degree. I am sure that my outdoor kennel dogs know when we are up and about and that the day has started when the lights go on and the radio plays. With their keen ears they might even hear a mumbled 'Good morning'.

Returning to the 'staying with friends' scenario, we gain information from sounds and sequences: 'I heard them go down to the kitchen and turn the radio on so it's OK for us to join them.' The dog may deduce the same thing but perhaps without the conclusion.

Try to Put Yourself in Their Place

It would be possible to sit in a house, listen to the sounds and make a fair guess at how the day is progressing. If you stop to think about it, listening and seeing is the only way your dog knows what is happening.

Dogs need a routine so that they know what is expected of them as well as what they can expect of you. The routine needs to be clear to the dog.

A Routine for Feeding

A good, practical example of my point is that when we set about feeding all our dogs we follow a time-honoured sequence.

The same dogs are fed at the same time, in the same order and eat in the same place every single day. The same signs and words are used as their meals are being prepared and distributed.

At feed time each dog goes to its appointed place of its own accord, whether a word has been spoken or not. One goes into the loo, one outside the front door, one in the hall and two in the kitchen. That is the first batch and the next two groups are dealt with in the same way.

There is no rush, no hassle, no jumping up. The slow eaters are assured of sufficient time and protected privacy to eat their dinner at the speed they choose, and the greedy ones can't filch a less dominant dog's meal. It makes for a relaxed and unchallenging environment.

The point of this example is not that the function runs smoothly (though that is important) but that each dog knows precisely what is going to happen.

Knowing what will happen next is a vital ingredient in the dog-whispering process. The dog gets so good at reading the signs that training and maintaining what it has learned become much easier.

A Routine for Training

The same sequences should be used in training: the same body language followed by the same spoken signal always in the same order. The order is as important as the content.

Dogs thrive on routine: they are much happier if the same kind of things happen at regular times as part of a regular routine that involves familiar sequences.

Training does not just happen on the training field but everywhere. The outcome is a dog that responds instantly to the most subtle signal because you have spent a lot of time broadening its understanding of the 'language'.

A Routine for Resting

Contrary to what a lot of people believe a dog does not need to be super-active all day long. In the wild it would have long periods of rest, and shorter periods of play and exercise. If it knows roughly when these different periods are going to happen and what signs will be given to herald them, the result will be a relaxed and contented dog. If it has a fair idea of what is going to happen from the moment it wakes up until bedtime it will settle happily into the pattern you have set.

A dog that lives without a recognisable routine is an unhappy dog.

It goes without saying that a contented dog is much more likely to be a well-behaved dog.

My life is fairly easy to plan because, although I have a certain amount of work to do each day, it doesn't particularly matter when I do it. My dogs are my priority and setting and keeping schedules or routines for resting, exercise and feeding is, happily, a simple matter.

Multiply by Fifteen

We have fifteen dogs that need exercise, training, grooming and generally looking after so there has to be a system for everyone's sake.

For fifteen years my wife and I have earned our living by demonstrating our dogs' skills, so their well-being is central to all we do. We share the work that has to be done but we keep to our own areas of expertise.

Our dogs go out for exercise at set times each day. I use a four-wheel drive to take batches of them to the set-aside training field. The vehicle is divided into two kennels. The same dogs go into the same kennel in the same order, through the same door, in the same way. All I have to do is point towards the door and they do the rest.

A dog does not need hours of exercise – though, of course, it will happily cope with long walks. Our dogs have two or three short breaks in the garden plus a hard running session in a very large field.

A long walk on a restricting lead is better than nothing, but only just. Dogs need periods of freedom, they need to run and do what dogs do naturally.

The energetic exercise session follows a routine. Ten minutes of do-as-you-please, to warm up the muscles, followed by twenty minutes of hard running combined with training, followed by another thirty minutes of please-yourself ambling and sniffing.

Quality is much more valuable than quantity, but it benefits the dog if the exercise follows a routine in that it happens at more or less the same time every day and lasts at least half an hour.

When I worked on a farm my dogs worked much harder than this, but now they are all older and older dogs need enough rather than too much.

If it is pouring with rain we give the exercise session a miss. I don't like walking in torrential rain and neither do many dogs.

It always annoys me when I see someone
so obsessed that they drag their poor dog around
wet and boring streets on a lead just because
their schedule says they should.

In short, it benefits a dog if all the events in its day-to-day life follow a routine, but not so slavishly that the whole thing becomes boring for human and dog.

Grooming: the Great Cure

This is a good place to talk about grooming. Grooming does a lot more for your dog than simply keeping its fur and skin in good condition.

Dogs are very much social animals and grooming allows for an affectionate and relaxing period of interaction that does wonders for your relationship. It is a good time, too, for checking your dog's well-being. Any strains or lumps and bumps will much more likely be discovered during a grooming session.

I use this time as a bonding opportunity, talking softly all the while and heaping praise on the dog's head.

Make grooming a part of your routine and put grooming periods after training sessions, especially those that did not go as well as you hoped.

After any kind of stress, grooming provides a reassurance, ˌtood by your dog, that all is still well. The action of groom-ˌhing and your dog will rapidly become much more ˌAs an added bonus, grooming will reduce your stress

ˌthere was a better way to win a dog's affection than by ˌhg, then I have yet to see it. Puppies, especially those that ˌust left their mother, love grooming as it goes some way to ˌace the attention that she would have shown them.

ˌI would groom a young puppy outdoors where it can see people coming past the garden. Or if it is nervous of open spaces, do it where you walk. This way there is a double benefit: you are giving your puppy a new experience as well as keeping within a routine.

If you have a very young puppy that has recently left its mother and appears to be unhappy in the room you chose for it to sleep in, groom it there just before it goes to bed and when you come down in the morning. This logic applies to anywhere your puppy finds frightening, indoors or out.

If we could have conversations with dogs we could tell them that a certain room or place is not so bad. As we can't, use grooming as loving communication and a fear-remover.

Socialising

Some of our dogs live outside and would not normally see the inside of a house but we think it important for them to socialise with us so they take it in turns to come in and experience an evening in front of the TV.

It teaches them to be civilised and avoids the possibility of boredom.

Outdoor Kennels

Dogs that live outside keep just as fit as indoor dogs, even in very cold weather. Our kennels are insulated, and the floors are a couple of feet deep in fresh straw. Each has a generous concrete run. In the summer they are shaded by Russian vine and screened with green garden netting.

An outside kennel is invaluable for those occasions on which your dog decides to roll in something absolutely disgusting.

In some ways I think dogs like the quiet privacy an outside kennel affords, but don't leave them out there for too long unless they have the company of another dog – and even then keep an eye on the time.

Our old dog Bob would not thank me for taking him indoors. He was born in a barn and has spent his whole life in quiet, straw-filled kennels. The noise from radio and television plus the warmth from central heating sends him to the door after less than an hour.

Problems Indoors

When your puppy is young, get it used to visitors coming and going. Puppies learn social skills remarkably quickly. Teach yours to behave well as it may be that your guests aren't as keen on dogs as you are.

I can't think of anything worse than a dog that worries guests sitting at the dinner table for scraps unless it is the guest who decides to give them some.

The easiest way to avoid this is not to do it. Once started, your dog will believe that your meals will always be shared with it – after all, you invited it to do so last time.

> *Dogs respond to the situation and the location.*

So don't start it! I never beg for any of my dogs' food and I most certainly do not like them looking for some of mine.

This is why it is a good idea for your dog to think it is as normal to be in the kitchen when guests are eating as it is to be in the room with them.

> *Beware of young children in high chairs – especially if the chair isn't very high. Small children delight in chucking food over the edge and watching pet dog eagerly eat it. A habit will form that is hard to break.*

A lot of problems happen indoors. The space is relatively small and you are all closer to each other than you would be outdoors.

Perhaps the most annoying is the dog that falls in love with your guest's leg. 'More tea, Vicar?' does not have the same polite ring if he or she is trying to avoid an amorous dog's persistent attentions.

Or there is the dog that happily lets someone in but won't let them out. Or the one that decides to sniff people continually when they do not want to be sniffed. Then there is the dog that loves visitors so much that it leaps up to kiss their faces when they come into the house. If it is a Great Dane or a German Shepherd the experience could be quite daunting. Even assurances of just how friendly Bonzo really is will give little peace of mind.

I could give a wonderfully comprehensive, behaviourist's answer to all of these problems but the common-sense solution is to put your dog in the kitchen five minutes or so before your guests arrive. In this way the problems have been prevented.

Will the dog be worried about being in the kitchen? No, not if you teach it that this is its normal place.

Many dogs will be fine when visitors are with you, but if you are not entirely sure of their behaviour, the kitchen awaits.

A good tip is to introduce your dog to the guests and then put it in another room, gradually increasing the time your dog spends with those visiting you.

Telling your visitors that friend dog is territorial is tantamount to admitting that you have no control over it.

Don't allow your dog to control the indoor space. You will notice if it starts to do this because it will place itself between you and any visitor, or will stand in strategic places, like doorways or corridors, making it difficult for people to pass.

Don't encourage your dog to jump on to the furniture by actively patting the chair and saying, 'Up.' It can take command of that chair because you have given it permission to do so.

I have been into houses in which the dog would not allow a human to sit on the chair that his mistress or master had given to him.

Turning a Blind Eye

If your dog slides up on to an acceptable old armchair you can turn a blind eye. This is quite different in the eyes of the dog because you did not tell it to get 'up' so 'get down' is not contradictory. However, if your dog is the dominant type, it is best to keep it off the furniture altogether.

The blind-eye approach is a good one because you retain control over the occupation of the chair.

Bad habits become so entrenched that they are difficult to break. It is much easier to prevent problems by early and correct training.

A behavioural problem is one that is so embedded in the dog that escaping from it will represent a major task often requiring a vet with behavioural skills to work on the problem.

They will need to see the dog and ask many questions about its history. Even then the reason for the problem might still be difficult to find and the cure, if possible, could take a long time. As time is money, get ready for a big bill as well.

Who Has Been Sleeping on My Bed?

This is a good place to mention dogs sleeping on your bed. It is not allowed in our house for comfort reasons and because we have lots of dogs.

My cousin has found a great compromise: he has put two comfortable cushions just outside his bedroom door. He leaves the door open but his two little dogs sleep contentedly outside on the landing. It works well because they know where he is and probably understand that he can't go in or out without attracting their attention.

In the past I have allowed dogs to sleep on my bed but I have never met one that is content with just its fair share of the bed.

When I am away doing demonstrations I take a caravan in which the dogs and I live. There are usually seven dogs in the show. When it comes to bedtime I set up a double bed and we share it. On a chilly March night I am usually the only human on the site who doesn't complain of the cold. The dogs all have the wit to know that this only happens on special occasions.

I also have a purpose in allowing them to sleep with me: when we wake up we will be performing together in front of several thousand people, and sleeping together cements a bond like nothing else.

The lady who owned our little Sheltie before we did allowed it to sleep with her and good luck to them. All they had in the world was each other and I can't think of anything more comforting for them both.

Little Gem doesn't sleep on the bed any more but because she, too, is an old lady now she has a sofa in my study. I have heard no complaints.

Barking

If your dog barks at a burglar and drives him off before he pinches the family silver, it receives gratitude and much appreciation. If it responds in the same way to the window cleaner – who appears to be doing much the same thing as the burglar – there is consternation.

The problem is difficult for the dog and more so for you. I wonder how many friendly neighbours have become less keen on you because they have been kept awake by your dog?

Barking, or rather curing barking, can be the most difficult problem there is. Dogs bark naturally but persistent barking is learned. A dog that is not checked early will develop a real penchant for persistent or 'nuisance' barking.

As we have dogs in outside kennels at the front of our house, plus more kennels at the back, barking is passed on like a relay.

It is normal for a dog to bark when someone walks past in the street. It will also bark when the postman approaches, having heard him long before you are aware of him. This is acceptable but prolonged barking is another matter.

A Cry for Help?

Dogs bark for several reasons. An old dog might bark because it has a medical condition or cognitive decline.

One of my old dogs will bark during the night in a particularly monotone way. There seems to be no trigger for this. It is highly likely that he is sleeping more in the day and suffers a disturbed sleep pattern at night. I call out of the window to him and he stops.

My call seems to reassure him. It is possible that the ageing process is causing some disorientation.

Reassurance that I am there, rather than a telling-off, seems to be the answer.

Very young puppies will bark and whine when you leave them because they don't want you to go. Dogs learn quickly that barking attracts your attention.

Shouting is Human Barking

As tempting as it might be, the wrong way to treat this is to shout at your dog. The first few times you shout will interrupt the barking but, after a pause, it will start again. Your dog might even believe that you have joined in and bark all the louder.

Your response, delivered as a reprimand, might be totally acceptable to your dog because it achieved its objective in attracting your attention.

However, it might make your dog give you a wide berth because it did not understand why you were shouting, which is not what you wanted to achieve.

On no account should you smack your dog: this will make it frightened of you and will hamper every other part of your training.

There is no one-size-fits-all remedy for the problem of persistent barking, but if you watch your dog carefully you will be able to see what kind of barking it is.

Please Don't Leave Me

Let's start with the young puppy. When you leave him he delivers a mix of barks and whines. He is saying, in essence, 'Please don't leave me.'

The kindest thing appears to be to take him with you – tempting for the tender-hearted. What it will achieve is a puppy that won't let you out of its sight.

Bedtime is slightly different: if you don't mind a dog in your room you can always take it up with you. In your bedroom it is far less likely to bark because it knows you are close by. Then you have the choice of letting your dog sleep in the bedroom for ever, or teaching it to sleep in the kitchen once it has grown out of the puppy stage. The latter can work, sometimes quite easily.

Dogs go through a 'sensitive' period that starts at around twelve weeks and lasts to around six months when sexual maturity begins. It can be considered a super-learning period.

Most dogs calm down considerably at two years old. Because your dog is older it will be less fretful and by then, because it has been in the bedroom, it will know where you are. Although I have done it successfully several times, I ought to point out that there is a risk to this two-stage process: 'luxury' dog, accustomed to the very best sleeping arrangements, might just expect this delicious habit to go on for ever.

If you are going out you obviously can't take your dog everywhere with you so you will need to make sure it doesn't bark incessantly when it is left. A good tip is to shut the front door, as though you have gone, and then stand quietly and listen. If the dog barks just a few times, it is learning. If it carries on, you have a problem.

Time It

My brother has a custom-built pen in his garage that he uses for his twelve-week-old German Shepherd. The dog sleeps in his son's bedroom but he leaves very early for work so there is a two-hour gap before my brother gets out of bed.

When the puppy was left in the kitchen on his own, he barked and howled so much that nobody managed to sleep. We agreed on an experiment. Before my nephew left for work he would put the puppy into the pen with a supply of toys, plenty of water to drink and, of course, his normal doggy bed. The toys were smeared with peanut butter. My brother's job was to time how long the pup kicked up a fuss.

The first morning it whined, half-heartedly, for five minutes, then was quiet for the next two hours. As the week progressed the period of whining decreased.

Timing the whining is a good way to test
if your puppy is learning.

The Plastic Bottle

The example above is, of course, about anxiety at a human's departure. If your dog barks and whines when you are in the next room, try the method I discovered some years ago.

I used a plastic bottle half-full of pebbles and shook it abruptly at the puppy as soon as it started whining or barking. It is like tapping on a window to stop a dog in the garden from barking. It's a new sound, one that the dog can't easily identify. And what makes it more effective is that often the dog can't make out straight away where the sound is coming from.

Because it doesn't know what it is, the dog pays attention long enough to stop what it is doing. If this aid is used regularly and promptly, especially at the puppy stage, the dog will remember it and the effect will last. If, later, the dog begins to develop a barking or whining habit, rattle the stone-filled bottle and add a fierce, 'NO!' You will need to shake the bottle immediately the noise starts if it is to be effective. My experience has been that this method works very well indeed – so much so that the rattling soon becomes redundant. It's usually enough just to show the bottle.

> *Dogs are very good at remembering the things they don't like.*

Once a puppy had got used to this treatment, the bottle-rattling proved useful for stopping other unwanted activities, both indoors and out.

There are also special collars on the market that cure excessive barking. The dog's barking activates either a mild electric shock, a burst of citronella spray or an ultrasonic tone. Do check with your vet, though, before using such a device because it is not a panacea for all ills and takes no account of what might be causing the barking or what the dog's reaction might be. I have never used such a thing but have seen other trainers who do. I much prefer a natural and friendlier way of training my dogs. I have noticed that dogs trained this way become robotic in their response.

There is also a method (much loved by behaviourists) called 'counter conditioning', which essentially means diverting your dog's attention from barking towards something else. For instance, every time your dog starts to bark, you teach it to pick up, say, a 'chew'.

To my mind this sounds like an overly complicated method and the time it takes would best be spent on achieving the prime objective.

Barking is far more likely in a dog that is bored and left on its own for too long. As I have said repeatedly throughout this book, a dog that has as much attention paid to its mental as well as its physical needs will be less likely to develop behavioural problems.

A rescue dog, especially an older one, could prove a more difficult proposition because as the new owner you will have no idea when, how or why the barking habit developed.

Territorial barking is hard to correct because the dog receives confirmation of the success of its action daily. It barks at the postman and the postman goes away.

One of our dogs barks when the postman comes for an entirely different reason: he likes the postman. The way to stop him barking is to open the door so that he can run out and enjoy a greeting. It might be worth trying this yourself, especially if you have a very young puppy because it is far less likely to bark at callers if it has a better idea of who they are.

You would be wise, though, to check first whether it is love or dislike before trying this remedy with your dog.

Chewing

Barking and chewing are closely related, as both are the product of boredom or being left alone. All dogs chew at the puppy stage. Some continue, but most will grow out of it. The secret is to channel the chewing so that they only nibble away at the acceptable.

Do not make the mistake of giving them an old pair of your slippers reckoning that because they smell of you the gift will be received with enthusiasm. Puppies do not know the difference between old and brand new, so you will start a habit that may lead to the extinction of the slipper in your house.

Toys

Now I come to the hardest word in this book for me to write. I don't know if it is prejudice, time-worn custom or a refusal to move with the times, but as a trainer, the word 'toy' makes me cringe. I just cannot imagine a trainer giving a young sheepdog a 'toy'. The word is not exactly forbidden but it is certainly frowned upon by a nurturer of working dogs. Perhaps it is just the name that irks: sheepdogs on farms don't 'play', they 'work'.

Perhaps their work tires them to such a degree that they don't need toys.

If any of my sheepdog associates read this book I shall never work again!

But as I don't rely on them for a living any more – here goes . . .

There are several safe toys on the market that are designed to be chewed. Some have a hollow that can be filled with tasty treats. Some squeak, while others, such as rawhide chews, are both durable and tasty. Puppies undoubtedly love them and munch on them with gusto. Most can be smeared with peanut butter, which should make them even more attractive to a dog.

I must confess that dogs like them and many owners swear by their usefulness. So, if I am objective, I have to admit that at certain times they are a good idea.

Better by far that your puppy should chew one than do what one of ours did, which was to denude a corner of the wall of its plaster.

Older dogs enjoy these toys as much as puppies do. The only possible disadvantage I can see is that it might encourage your dog to see anything on the floor as something new to chew. Therefore, as a cautionary note, be careful not to leave anything dangerous within your dog's reach.

A great way to prevent your dog from chewing is to make sure that it is not left on its own for long periods of time.

A Safe Environment

If you are going to leave your dog, do make sure that its environment is both safe and comfortable.

It was not uncommon with some of the careless farmers I knew for puppies to hang themselves because a nail in the wall or some other protuberance caught the jumping puppy's collar. Take the collar off if there appears to be even the smallest risk.

Because young dogs can and do jump, make sure there are no bleach bottles, antifreeze or other dangerous items anywhere near them – and that includes the draining board which should also be kept clear.

Antifreeze is apparently palatable to dogs, as well as being poisonous. A friend of mine lost his much-loved Boxer because he left it in his garage without checking first to see if there were any dangerous substances within the dog's reach. It ate some strong glue, which rapidly set in its throat. No more detail is needed.

If arsenic tastes nice, a dog will eat it!

Chapter Twenty

Jumping Up and Pulling

When a dog jumps up it is usually an enthusiastic greeting. If the ground is muddy and you have your best clothes on, you may not be very pleased to receive it. If your dog weighs in at five stone and the focus of its attention is infirm or a small child, the 'greeting' may become dangerous.

It might well be that, quite unintentionally, you, or a member of your family, encouraged the jumping up.

Chase or wrestling games will encourage dogs to jump up and the dog will regard it as an acceptable part of playing.

When we call a dog most of us pat our legs to encourage it to come back. If the patting action is done on the stomach, or higher, then this acts as an invitation to jump up. Holding a ball or a treat in the air will also persuade the dog to jump to get whatever is in your hand.

I trained one of my star dogs to jump up at the end of the show as a kind of affectionate finale. He does it with such bounce that all four feet hit home with considerable force. That was a big mistake on my part.

I think that the margin between stable and unstable shrinks dramatically at the point of jumping, especially if the dog is inclined to mouth in its excitement.

Of course there is a theory that puppies jump up at their mother to encourage her to regurgitate food but I would discount this as any dog knows the difference between the height of its mother and that of a human. Besides which, the puppy's search for regurgitated food involves a much more complicated series of head- and body-turning movements.

Jumping can also
be part of the attack mode.

I remember treading accidentally on my dog's foot during a show. It made him yelp. To make amends I patted my stomach so that he would jump up to receive an apologetic cuddle. As I bent my head forwards he inserted his teeth in the end of my nose. Very painful and entirely my own fault.

It is altogether safer if you teach your dog not to jump up.

So, How Do You Do It?

A lot of dog trainers push out a knee to meet the jumping dog. This is fine if you are an expert – and big and strong enough – but the timing and force have to be judged just right. If it is too hard the dog can be intimidated beyond intention. If it is too soft the dog thinks you are playing and its attempts to jump will increase, as will its vigour.

> *If your timing is wrong you will encourage the dog to jump again.*

This type of preventive action carries too many risks with it and, though I have done it myself, I would not recommend it to you as the best method.

The other physical method is to allow the dog to jump up, hold its front legs to you, and then slide your foot so that the sole of your shoe is just above its back foot. You then exert gradual pressure on its foot. Eventually the dog deduces that jumping up brings about a pain in its foot. It doesn't like it, so the jumping ceases.

There is no need to put undue pressure on the foot as too much could hurt your dog and discourage in all directions.

There is a disadvantage with this method too: as your head has to be in a position to see the dog's back foot this also means that your face is unhealthily close to the dog's mouth.

Children Should Not Train Dogs

Preventing jumping up, by whatever method you choose, should only be done by a strong and totally aware adult. Children should not, under any circumstances, be allowed to do this because dogs recognise strength and authority and are likely to regard a child as being lower in the pack order.

Letting a child do this is tantamount to inviting the dog to bite.

Children too often tend to try to overpower dogs physically, especially puppies, believing that this and an overloud voice is the way to gain authority. Neither of these treatments is effective and could easily increase aggression in a dog. In fact, is likely to do so.

If your dog has learned to respond to the noisy shaking of a plastic bottle, half-full of coins or pebbles (which I recommended to stop barking), then try this as an option: one sharp shake as the jump starts should do the trick.

My recommended method is 'withdrawal'. The minute your dog starts to jump, turn away from it, fold your arms and ignore it completely. Make an obvious and overstated movement, and if your dog tries to lick your hand withdraw it in a dramatic fashion.

Once your dog has stopped jumping, praise it. You will probably need to do this several times, on different occasions, but before very long your dog will learn that jumping up is not a way to endear itself to you.

This is a good time to repeat that training should be done by one person using the same sequences of body language and always the same words.

If you have an adult rescue dog, past the training stage, then withdrawal must be the favoured option.

You will not know what sort of training methods have been used on the dog or what sort of person carried them out. As a general rule it is probably safe to assume that they became rescue dogs because their previous owners were not able to train them.

A harsh judgement perhaps but probably true in most cases.

If your dog does not respond to any of the treatments I have recommended here, which is highly unlikely, then buy a head halter. This device is gentle and effective.

The halter is best used for taking your dog out for a walk when there is a danger of meeting small children.

The Boy on the Lead

When I was a little boy of around eight years old I volunteered to take the Dalmatian that lived next door out for a walk. The owners were elderly and probably not up to dealing with a strong dog. I managed to get it to the park but coming back down a hill, its pulling increased my momentum beyond controlling. The dog dragged me down the slope with my face bouncing off the pavement. It showed no awareness of my predicament even though I must have been pulling its lead reasonably hard. Looking back, I would imagine that the dog went out so rarely that when it did it was completely beyond control.

Now I know that the harder you pull on the lead, the greater will be the dog's effort to outpull you. It has no appreciation of its handler's struggle.

In our collection of leads there are no choke collars. Taking a dog out on a lead should not be a contest but rather a pleasure for both participants.

The best place for initial lead training is the garden where it is private. None of us likes to be seen being hauled along the street by a struggling dog, and other people's comments do little to help what should be a peaceful and trust-winning exercise. Most dog owners who receive some sort of sarcastic comment will react by trying to demonstrate their control over their dog by being overly physical.

Put some time in to the process in the garden because that is the one place where you can take the lead off without worrying that your dog will run away.

Try it by degrees. Clip the lead on, then take it off. Don't worry about going anywhere. As your dog gets used to the feel of the lead, make the session last just a little bit longer.

If your dog dances around showing signs of distress, take the lead off.

Once it begins to show that it is more at ease, walk on a few paces. Don't rush and most certainly do not pull your dog. Be prepared to stand still for several minutes until your dog shows a willingness to move on. Gradually it will stop worrying about the thing 'tied round its neck'.

Sometimes when I see people in the street struggling to hold on to their badly trained dog, which I know they've had for a couple of years, I wonder whether just a couple of weeks of patience would not be preferable to two years of struggle.

If your dog continues to pull, stand still until it stops, and only when it stops should you allow it to move on again.

With a puppy, don't inflict a double shock by putting collar and lead on together. Put the collar on first and let your puppy become totally accustomed to it before you try the lead.

Once your dog has learned how to walk nicely in the garden, you can then venture out on to the street.

If you have tried my recommended 'walk on' exercise, alternating between lead and no lead, you will find walking your dog on the lead much easier.

Chapter Twenty-one

Find a Good Vet

Money, Money, Money

Several years back, I was working at the Milky Way, the theme park at Clovelly in North Devon. My job there was to do sheepdog demonstrations, plus all sorts of other things, like running a sheepdog breeding and training centre. Some of our lambs looked poorly so I called the vet in. After he had looked at the lambs and treated them, I walked him back to his car. On the way I asked him if he could give me some advice on one of my dogs. I told him that her name was Misty and that she had some sort of problem with her back legs. She was about seven months old and was being trained for the shows.

Instead of running with a smooth action she placed her back legs together, so that one leg supported the other, and sort of 'bunny-hopped'. At first I thought it was due to some kind of twist or strain and that she would get over it, but it didn't get any better.

It took me about as long as it took you to read the last paragraph to tell him this. He outlined three possible problems, got into his car and drove off.

About a week later I received a bill. In my book, that is not the sign of a good vet. The next day I went to another practice and showed Misty to the vet there. He was charming, listened carefully to all I had to say, then X-rayed her.

She had a malformed hip. He knew a skilled veterinary surgeon in Exeter and suggested that Misty be taken to see him.

My wife took her to the surgery for a pretty complicated operation. We were told to rest her for about six weeks and then gently ease her to fitness, starting with the shortest lead walks imaginable and gradually increasing their length. In the seventh week I unclipped her lead and off she went, trotting awkwardly – but trotting. A week later, she was bringing sheep back from very short distances. A month afterwards she was running half-mile laps of the training sheep field, not gracefully but strongly.

That all happened about seven years ago. It was hard to describe the joy I felt at her transformation and every time she goes round the sheep I am revisited by that same joy together with a feeling of real gratitude.

She can't jump into the back of our truck – I have to lift her – and after a long run her back leg trembles, but we have her and she is fulfilled, doing what nature and breeding shaped her for.

The vet who diagnosed her problem and treated her after her surgery and the surgeon who performed the operation will have my gratitude for as long as I live. They reversed what seemed a hopeless situation, and to see the skill of their work and the rewards for Misty fills me with admiration.

When we moved to the Midlands we had to find another vet. We thought it would be difficult to find one as good as most of those in Devon.

One day I received a baptism application from a couple in a nearby village. I noticed from the form they had filled in that he was a vet. When I met him at the church I warmed to him immediately because of his quiet, gentle manner.

A short time later I took one of my dogs along to his surgery. Jack had been having severe fits and their frequency had increased. I thought that it must be some form of epilepsy but after examining him and asking me a host of questions, Richard told me that he thought it was actually a kind of sexual frustration and that the fits had probably increased because some of my bitches were coming into season.

The Non-risk Prognosis

He then suggested what I considered to be an inspired line of treatment. First he would treat Jack with a drug that would temporarily have the same effect as castration, without the risk of surgery. Our job was to watch him for two weeks to see if he had any more fits. He didn't, so the operation went ahead. Jack had no more seizures. It had been, as Richard suspected, a case of fits caused by sexual frustration.

A Good Listener

Richard has the real gift of being a good listener and his clients must be aware that he knows how they feel about their pets. I sense too that he keeps his knowledge right up to date by reading the latest works.

When he came to our house to administer booster injections to our fifteen dogs, he would also give each one a thorough physical check-up, taking time to do it properly. He is well versed in behavioural problems and when he heard I was writing this book he lent me a copy of *Behavioural Medicine*.

That is my idea of a good vet!

When my wife and I moved to Wales our first task was to find another good vet. We asked local people who have dogs for their recommendations and then went to see the vet they liked. So far, though, I have not found one that I am totally happy with. In rural districts, vets tend to join together to form a larger practice, which becomes dominant in the area. In my view, it is the clients who can lose out in this situation. Unlike with my previous vet and his nursing staff, who knew every detail about each of my dogs, with a larger practice where there are several vets, you never know which one you'll get to see. Continuity and care are to my mind the potential casualties.

Used to the superior skills Richard offered, the merely competent will not do for me. My search goes on . . .

The Right Knowledge

It is vital to consult a good vet who understands small animals. I have had vets in the past who were used to large animals like horses, sheep and cows, but it is not the same.

A vet should have a good 'bedside manner', be a good listener and appreciate just how important a much-loved pet is to their client. They should also be up to date on research and treatment.

I remember years ago having to give a lecture to the fellows of a zoological society. I was terrified because they probably knew much more about the subject than I did.

I intended to talk about gorillas, tigers and pandas. I kept rehearsing and worrying. There was no need because my work as a wildlife artist had equipped me to see the things that they had not, especially in the area of animal behaviour.

Many of my art commissions were for the World Wildlife Fund, the Royal Society for the Protection of Birds and the Royal London Zoological Society (among others), so a high degree of expert knowledge about habitat and behaviour as well as physical detail was essential. As an artist specialising in animal portraits, I am able to see much more keenly and that ability has been invaluable to me as a dog trainer.

I felt a lot less daunted once I realised that what I was saying was new to them. I was impressed then when my vet Richard understood what I was saying about dog training and behaviour, as I had not met a vet before with that kind of 'outside' knowledge.

Behavioural problems can be a real concern, possibly needing medical intervention or remedial training, and it is important to be able to get an expert and qualified view. There are people called behaviourists but I, for one, would prefer to speak to a vet capable of giving holistic advice.

The vet I used in Devon was excellent at the kind of medical care you would expect, but often consulted *me* for behavioural problem-solving.

There is a systematic approach to dealing with behavioural

problems: it involves collecting a truthful history of the dog, then recommending a suitable treatment based on a wide knowledge of the possible causes of the problem.

A Shopping List

Here is my shopping list of the qualities I would look for in a good vet:

- Understands small animals

- Willing to help, in or out of normal hours, in the case of an emergency

- Up-to-date knowledge of behavioural problems

- Sympathetic listener, with a good 'bedside manner'

- A calm, quiet, gentle approach

- Takes sufficient time to fully understand the problem and does not rush through the procedure to get to the next fee-paying client

- Understands that he is dealing with your best friend

- Has a real gift for making the most accurate diagnosis possible

- Gives a full check-up every time your dog needs a booster injection

- Explains the treatment options available, with the possible consequences, risks and benefits

- Is capable of being upset

Most of all, look for someone who you can see is considering the long-term health of your dog rather than just responding to the immediate problem.

Chapter Twenty-two

Those You Have Loved and Lost

You might think this a very strange subject to include in a book like this, but the unthinkable happens. If you are like me and have had several dogs, you will know just how it feels when you lose your best friend.

The Bishop's Dog

What prompted me to write this chapter was a telephone conversation between my bishop's wife and me. They had just lost their much-loved dog and the bishop had just done what all owners may sadly have to do.

I asked her if he was all right. She told me how cut up about it he was. Bishops and vicars spend their lives dealing with loss, so you would think that the regularity of doing it would prepare them in some way. It doesn't.

When people lose a pet, it is obvious to everyone else that they are deeply upset. Often, though, they will tell you that their grief is silly 'because it was only a dog'.

Of course, they don't mean it. What they really mean is that perhaps other people find their grief hard to understand, and think they are being overly sentimental about something that somehow does not deserve it.

The trouble is that a dog's life, compared to our expected span, is short. It wasn't 'only a dog', but a great, dear and precious friend.

Down in Devon, amid a circle of trees on what used to be an estate of substance, is a small gravestone mourning the passing of some doggy friend. The date on the stone is 1830 but through it, and the love that prompted its making, he or she lives on.

It is perhaps even harder for someone who holds the Christian faith because the Bible appears to allow only humans a soul. But there is a lovely Sunday-school story about a dog.

God was naming all of the animals. As they followed Him, He gave each its name – Giraffe, Elephant, Monkey and so forth. Because there were so many animals, the naming went on for many days until there was just one left.

The animal had tears running down its face, so God asked it why it was crying. 'I haven't got a name,' it answered.

'Well,' said God, 'I was saving yours till last for you shall be man's best friend and therefore need a very special name.

'Your name shall be God spelt backwards.'

At primary school assembly, children often ask me if their rabbit, hamster, guinea pig, dog or cat will go to heaven. I answer, 'Yes', reasoning that if God is love, then love draws no barriers. Did the donkey that carried Jesus go to heaven? Of course it did!

I have buried much-loved dogs and marked their places with the most beautiful rhododendrons I could find. Every time I go outdoors I remember the sorrow, the acute pain and the absolute joy of having had him or her as my very real friend.

A few years ago a television crew came to film me working my dogs at the Milky Way theme park. When we had finished the action, the reporter asked if I would answer one last question.

'Is it on or off the record?' I asked.

'Off,' he replied.

He wanted to know the difference between a dog and a member of my congregation. I really should have checked to see if their equipment was still running, but I didn't.

My answer was indiscreet. I told him that dogs were more intelligent and, after a pause, went on to say that dogs never argue, are never spiteful and that humans could learn much about love and loyalty from them. In fact, I said, warming to my theme, the world would be a better place if humans could develop these doggy attributes.

That night I saw the interview on TV and wilted at the thought that the very next day I would be preaching to the congregation in question. I consoled myself with the fact that at least the reporter had been responsible and included my entire answer rather than picking out only the most provocative parts.

Sunday morning came along with my time to preach. As I spoke to the congregation, I watched their expressions carefully, fully expecting to see some sort of annoyance on their faces.

There was none. In the end I just had to ask if they had seen the television the night before. They had! To a man, they had.

'Did I offend you?' I asked.

A man answered in the soft Devon drawl I had come to love: 'No m'dear, 'tis true.'

The congregation nodded their unanimous agreement.

Absolute, unswerving love and loyalty are what dogs give to their human friends, so it is no small wonder that we miss them so acutely when they are no longer there.

Dogs grieve, too. When I lost one of my best dogs the others looked into the distance as though they were waiting for him to return. They grieve for their humans too.

There is the story of a dog that lived with its master in Tokyo. Each day professor Eisaburo Ueno would go to work on the train, and every day, when he came back, his dog would be waiting for him on the platform. Then the professor died at work. The dog, an Akita named Hachiko, continued to come to the platform every day for eleven years, ever hopeful of his master's return. The Japanese were so impressed by the dog's loyalty that they erected a bronze statue of him at Shibuya station as well as naming an entrance to the station after him.

Love is a Two-way Thing

There is also a touching story of a Skye Terrier, known as Greyfriars Bobby. Bobby's owner, John Gray, died in 1858 and was buried in the cemetery of Greyfriars kirk in the old town of Edinburgh.

Bobby lived for a further ten years and is said to have spent his life sitting on his master's grave.

In 1867, when it was pointed out that an un-owned dog should by law be put down, the Lord Provost of Edinburgh, Sir William Chambers, paid for a renewal of Bobby's licence, making him the responsibility of the city council.

Small wonder that the loss of a beloved dog is so keenly felt.

Guilt

Something practical can be done. Perhaps the very worst thing about bereavement is guilt. 'I wish I'd done or not done this or that'; 'I wish I'd been kinder'; 'I could have done that if I'd really tried'.

Perhaps we would be better served if we paid our attention to the dog while it is still alive.

I have noticed that at human funerals, the grief is always more intense, and confused, if there is a real reason for guilt to be felt.

If you are a less than saintly dog owner, you will know, with precision, just what I'm saying. It will strike a tuning fork that resonates in your memory and your conscience.

If you have tremendous foresight you can start when your dog is young. However, it is more likely that, as your dog starts to age and you realise time is limited, you will make a resolution to treat it with the utmost kindness, to give it the best possible life you can manage.

Guilt is like a large, black bird that not only roosts in the conscience but pecks at it for ever.

Think how much easier it would be if you could look back and say to yourself, 'I really did the very best for my dog.' You will still be sad, of course, but at least the sadness will be wholesome rather than tinged with the bitter taste of regret.

When I was a small boy I nagged my mother to allow me to have a dog. Eventually, after a lot of effort from me, she weakened. I had a little mongrel with a hint of Spaniel. My life was complete and I was as happy as a sandboy – whatever 'sandboy' means. The days were endless with sheer enjoyment.

One day after I had gone to school, the dog kept barking. My mother's solution was to open the gate and let it out. It ran in the direction of my school but as it crossed the road it was run over.

When I got there it was no more than a flattened pelt in the road. To a young boy the snuffing out of something precious and vibrant is deeply horrifying. I loved that little dog not just for what it was but also for how it rounded out my life. Even now, towards my dotage, I can feel the echoes of that day. When I reproached my mother, she pointed out that, 'It was only a dog.'

Perhaps that defensive one-liner, delivered on the spur of an unthinking moment, has been overly nurtured by me and turned into a more damning remark than it was ever intended to be.

I was lucky enough to marry a girl who loves animals as much as I do. We set about having dogs that would not be exiled to an unkind road if they barked.

That bereavement is with me still.

If my clergy friends read this they will point out my theological error, but this is what I believe and hope for: that the day I die I shall see a cob cottage on the edge of the moor. As I open the gate a host of dogs and cats (and geese, ducks and sheep) will rush out to meet me – including that little mongrel. Then I shall hear laughter from inside the cottage, as if a wonderful tea party is going on, and all those I have loved and lost will be there.

Impossible? Wishful thinking?

No. Heaven is complete, not incomplete.

Disloyalty?

Sometimes after losing a loved dog the thought of getting another may seem like an act of disloyalty.

When my wife lost her Yellow Labrador, I thought that after a time I could introduce another and that this would end, or at least soften, her sadness.

I purchased the best-looking Labrador I could find and took it home. When she saw it, all the old memories were stirred up and she was deeply upset.

I had to take the new dog back. It was perhaps an insensitive thing to do on my part, but I'd thought I was helping. We did not have another dog for quite a few years as a result of my wrong solution.

Getting a new dog is not disloyal to the one you have lost. The new dog will not erase the memory of the old one or displace it in your heart.

Some people wait for a while before they get a new dog, but others (sensibly, I think) get a new one as their dog starts to age. It is quite amazing how a puppy can give a new lease of life to an old dog, and you will avoid all of those feelings of disloyalty.

When Molly died I took great comfort from the fact that we had kept one of her puppies. It looks so much like her that every time I see her it is just like having Molly still. Is she the same as her mum? No, of course not. She is wonderfully different.

However you choose to do it, don't make the mistake of comparing your new dog to the old one. They will not be the same and you probably wouldn't like it if they were.

But who am I to comment?

When my wife read this chapter she pointed out that we have fifteen to lose; a dread we share. Samuel Butler wrote, ''Tis better to have loved and lost, than never to have lost at all.' I prefer Tennyson's version: ''Tis better to have loved and lost than never to have loved at all.' Oh, and by the way, the bishop now has another dog and what a little sweetie she is.

Chapter Twenty-three

The Sound of
One Hand Clapping

'A Very Fine Dog Indeed'

At the start of my dog-handling career I watched a training video of a famous Welsh sheepdog trialist working with a young dog. The various scenes covered the whole process from beginning to end.

The first stage sticks in my mind, like a burr in a dog's coat. It showed a young dog of around nine months old: I have never seen such a mad dog or such antics. It looked like a lost cause as it chased the sheep back and forth with neither rhyme nor reason. The commentator's confident closing remark was that, 'This dog will be a very fine dog indeed!' (It was not the verdict I would have given.)

I thought at the time that the dog would never make it. In fact, if it were mine, I wouldn't attempt to try.

Later in the video, the trainer showed the finished dog. It was calm, collected, totally together and exactly as he had predicted it would be. It followed his commands precisely, gently moving the sheep to where he wanted them to go.

It appeared to be a different dog and because I was cynical I wound the video back and took note of its markings to see if it really was the same one. It did not seem possible that the 'mad' dog I had seen earlier could have turned into such an assured expert.

The commentator's prediction was accurate beyond belief. I found this unlikely metamorphosis heartening. If he could bring about such a change, so could I.

If you follow the training method I recommend you will see as dramatic a change in your own dog. Dog whispering is neither mystical nor a form of alchemy but a procedure that works.

Graduation is not so much a date or a time in the training process but a happening. An awareness that something beyond reasonable expectation has occurred. Zen writings cite 'the sound of one hand clapping', which I understand as a sublime, and inexplicable, moment.

After you have worked through all of the specifics with your dog, something beyond the sum of all the parts occurs and quite remarkable changes can be observed. Like driving a car after clutch, accelerator and brake have ceased to be foreign bodies and you realise that you have just driven from one place to another without noticing.

The realisation that this day has been reached surprises even someone who has been through the process many times.

One of my dogs regards an exciting moment as 'bark-yourself-silly time'. I discovered that a cold stare not only stopped it barking but sent it scurrying away from the source of the silent reprimand. It was a clear demonstration of the developed understanding that can be conveyed without sound.

Often it happens during a quiet, without-training, mind-somewhere-else, stroll: you suddenly notice that your dog seems joined to you by some invisible string. The need to watch it all the time and the labour of doing so are removed. Your dog does what you want it to do on the basis of a glance.

When I am watching a football match between two top teams and a player, without looking up to check, passes, or flicks, the ball into an empty space and a team-mate, sensing the movement, is almost waiting for it, I find myself deeply impressed. What had actually happened was the result of them training together; their continual practice developed not only their technical skills but also their anticipation.

The first signal you send to your dog will not only achieve what was intended but will also 'flick a switch' that turns on its keen attention. Eventually it will anticipate your next move.

All it takes is for the dog to notice the things you don't know you are doing, but do every time, and it will begin to read you. Dogs read people much better than the other way round.

By now you will have achieved the understanding you have been aiming for – except that it will soon be obvious that your expectations have been exceeded to a degree that will surprise you.

I well remember my dog Bob and I reaching this stage and just how exhilarated I felt when I realised we could actually 'talk' to each other. I expect he felt the same thrill. It must be vexing to a dog, as much as it is to a human, when there is no understanding or rapport. The result was that we became like the two footballers anticipating the other's next move.

Life with your dog will become an effortless and totally enjoyable experience once the training has been happening long enough for an understanding to fully develop. It is worth remembering, though, that the training is never complete and that the learning process for both dog and owner never really ends.

Dog whispering works on all aspects of your relationship because it educates you as much as it trains your dog and makes both of you much more sensitive to the other's requirements. You will become aware of all sorts of things that you did not notice before.

I included a chapter on bereavement as a forceful reminder that nothing is for ever, that you need to make the most of one another in the time you have available. This is not because of some morbid preoccupation with mortality, but to encourage you to truly value one another.

It is in valuing that the real essence of dog whispering resides.

The ultimate objective of the intelligent dog trainer is not just to have their commands obeyed but to reach a level of understanding that makes the whole thing a satisfying experience for both animals.

Several years ago I heard, or read, that a dog's intelligence is equal to that of a five-year-old child. If the experts had worked with dogs rather than looking at them, I think they may have pushed their estimate up a little. A dog is not a human so it is unrealistic to compare in this way. A dog has a different intelligence, so understanding that difference, rather than comparing, is the real key to working well together.

I do not think of my dogs as just dogs but as my real friends. When people at my demonstrations express admiration at the precision of their work and ask what the secret is, I rarely respond totally truthfully because the answer would seem too simple. Audiences regard what they have seen as some kind of remarkable magic and, I suspect, think that few people have the necessary 'gift' to make such a thing happen.

They do, however, get one observation right every time when they remark that, 'The dogs were enjoying themselves.'

So, the answer to their question is surprisingly simple and was right under their noses all the time.

The secret is to love them more, and by loving learn to appreciate and understand the wonder of this creature we call 'dog'.

Chapter Twenty-four

My Notebook

I have included in this section all those points that did not warrant a chapter to themselves.

Assessment

This could be called the first objective look. When I am training someone else's dog I go through a series of checks that will give me an assessment of its likely strengths and weaknesses. I would not do this with a small puppy but with a dog nearer to six months old. With a young puppy all I can do is work on a kind of hunch because the puppy is not fully formed mentally or physically. There can be huge and unexpected changes as it grows.

Even when you know your dog, or think you do, it is still possible to be objective. It is, however, all too easy to make an emotional judgement that has very little to do with the truth. When I first went on a handler's training course the instructor asked me what my dog was like. I told her he was a tough, independent dog who could be quite wilful.

She took a quick look and then proceeded to tell me that my reading of him was quite wrong. He was, in her words, 'sensitive, very willing to please and as soft as butter'.

I was quite cross at the time, though I didn't show it, thinking to myself that she didn't know the first thing about a dog I had been working with successfully for some time. I was quite obviously right and she was wrong. (My opinion was actually more colourful than described here.)

That night I thought about what she had said and realised I had made judgements based not only on the wrong information but also on the basis of what I wanted the dog to be. A kind of idealisation. Because Bob was able to hold a herd of cows by standing in an open gateway and refusing them entry I had assumed he was tough by nature.

Courageous would have been more accurate. The fact that he was prepared to do such a brave thing showed he was, as she had said, 'willing to please'.

But surely the 'sensitivity' she had mentioned was absolutely wrong? No, she was right about that too. If I spoke to him softly he responded instantly, far more quickly than when I shouted. If my body language was slow and deliberate, rather than quick and jerky, he responded calmly.

At this stage in my career I'd figured I was pretty good at what I did, but the instructor's advice pointed to a lack of objectivity in my assessment.

I think we are all prone to projecting what we want *to be there on to what is* actually *there, and doing it so well that the wishful obliterates the reality. Love is blind both with dogs and people.*

The next day I looked objectively at Bob and what I saw prompted me to make a few adjustments to our training routine.

It is possible for you to look again at your dog and see what is truly there. Maybe the system I now use when I meet a dog that I am going to train for the first time will be helpful.

Try to think as a detective would when looking for clues.

- Take a fresh look at your dog: what sort of physique has it got? Is it long legged and slim, chunky and short, or just somewhere comfortably between?

- Does it delight in running?

- Is it quick and alert, enthusiastic?

- What does its expression tell you? Is it nervous or calm? Does it respond instantly?

- Can I spot weaknesses? How does the dog watch me? Is it nervously attentive, or at ease?

I write all of this down so that later I can check on accurate observations rather than relying on the selective nature of memory. After I have looked at the dog I ask myself some leading questions, first looking at what I have done in a general sense and then going on to the detail.

- Did I make a wrong assessment and did this affect the way I trained the dog?

- Did I read stubborn when I should have realised the dog was confused?

- Did I deliver fierce when it should have been calm?

- Did I give it freedom to do the things it really enjoyed doing?

- Was I working with it or against it?

- Was my behaviour compatible with the nature of the dog?

- How am I going to address what I now see objectively?

If a particular sequence in the training recommendations I have made is proving difficult, then change your approach to a slower, more patient one.

Working with Two or More Dogs

A lot of people own more than one dog. Even if two dogs are from the same litter their characters will be different, so they will need different styles of training.

The same methods still apply but you will need to adjust the way you do it. For instance, one dog might naturally be disposed to sitting and the other to either lying down or standing. One might favour hard running while the other, perhaps less energetic, might be fonder of the close work. Your success will be increased if you ensure that you include slightly more of what the dog prefers – in other words, if you work with, rather than against.

One Dog at a Time

You can only train one dog at a time, but when both are trained it is easy to work them both. If one dog is already trained it may help you to train the other. For example, a dog that already knows how to sit will, by its example, speed up teaching the other to do the same. But for most of the time you need to train each dog on its own.

If you are training two dogs, you will need to vary their commands. There are two very effective ways, that I know of, to do this. First, you can preface the command with the dog's name: for example 'Bob sit', 'Meg stand'. This method has the advantage of enabling you to direct the command at one dog. It has the added bonus of being understood by both dogs when you remove the name from the command. No name equals a joint command.

My preferred method, though, is to use a different language for each dog, which is much less complicated than it sounds. Because I only ever train one dog at a time it is the only one that, through exposure and repetition, responds to the language being used.

When I put the dogs together, each only obeys the language they have been trained in. Over the course of several years both dogs have usually learned to understand the other language but each still obeys only its own.

You do not need to speak the languages fluently as you only need to learn a few commands. My method of learning is to ask, say, a German friend to give me the phonetic version of 'sit', 'stand', 'stop' etc. The dog will take longer than you to understand the commands, so you will have more than enough time to practise the words, and even if you are only one word ahead of the dog you are in business.

In a sheepdog brace trial I would work in Welsh and English. Each language sounds completely different to the dog. 'Lie down' becomes 'Gore vath', 'Walk on slowly' becomes 'Ara deig' (both of these have been typed phonetically).

Different dogs prefer different languages: a timid dog will work better in French because the language is soft and soothing; a bold, tough dog will like German, as it is curt and full of authority.

Once both dogs are trained and start to work together, be careful that the loud voice you use to address the tough dog does not have a disturbing effect on the timid one. Here you have options: you can gradually soften the harsher of the two tones, or be prepared to comfort the most timid dog. Although the timid dog knows that the harsher command was not directed at it, there is a danger that the unaccustomed strength of the command will unsettle it.

My impression with timid dogs is that they think the fault is always theirs. I remember training a dog for a Swiss vet: we had a choice of two languages, as she lived on a border where both German and French were spoken. We chose French because it suited the nature of the dog.

One of my bitches responds to a North Welsh dialect and

another of the dogs works on more of a South Wales accent; when they work together they are quite able to distinguish the subtle difference between 'Diddy mar' and 'Derry mar' (again given phonetically).

When I tell Megan that she is a 'Cariad varch' (a little darling), she fully understands the complimentary nature of the words and revels in the praise. Dogs hear the sound, hence my phonetic spellings of the foreign command words.

'Singing' Commands

When I worked on farms in Devon I noticed that shepherds would use certain words, which they 'sang' rather than shouted. The practice is probably hundreds of years old. At the time I used them too, but did not really appreciate why. The sung words could be heard from one valley to another and were quite clear even from two miles away.

Instead of shouting, 'Here', the shepherd would sing, in a tenor pitch, 'Yer'; sometimes it would be stretched to 'Yeerr'; and at other times they would sing a repeat of 'Yer, yer, yer'.

As my old dog Bob grows deafer I use the 'yer' rather than the whistle for 'come' or 'here'. Even though the whistle is far louder he doesn't hear it, but he always hears the sung command.

*I would recommend the sung command
not only for a dog that is growing deaf but
also to attract any dog's attention.*

I used the sung command for a lemon and white Cocker Spaniel we once had. As she got older Sally became blind. Indoors, everything was fine providing we did not move any of the furniture. Outdoors, though, the problems were greater. Sally would still come off her lead for exercise, and for much of the time her mother, Penny, would nudge her away from snow- or water-filled drainage ditches. But in open spaces she would treat the sung commands as a kind of location finder so that she could stay close to me.

Those old Devon shepherds knew a thing or two, which is hardly surprising given that the skills of working with a dog have been passed down many generations.

Association

The Devon dialect word for a lamb is 'tib' but it was also used in other contexts. When shepherds wanted to make a dog alert, they would sing 'Tib, tib, tib'. This had the effect of concentrating the dog's mind on the task in hand.

Dogs often work by association: it may appear as though they not only understand the word itself but also the likely scenarios the word conjures up. With my first dog, Annie, the word 'tibs' seemed to have several implications.

'Tib' meant just one lamb whereas 'tibs' meant several. Now this all sounds highly unlikely: how would a dog know which task the word 'tib' refers to and how would it know the difference between one lamb and several?

I think it depends on where they are when they hear it. If the dog is behind sheep the association is made with the situation rather than the command. If the command is given next to the lambing field, the dog knows that it means, 'Go and see if they are all right.'

So, in some way the dog is combining what it has heard with what it sees and is interpreting the meaning of the call in relation to what is happening.

I have never tried it but think it highly likely that if a dog was given a dummy at the beginning of a walk it would quickly make the association between the dummy and commencement of a walk. More importantly, carrying the dummy would stop the dog pulling.

Distractions

You will not make much progress with the earlier stages of your training schedule if you do it in a crowded area full of distractions. Find a quiet place away from other dogs, especially the ill-trained ones. By a quiet place, I mean completely out of sound and sight of other dogs.

Later, your dog will have learned to focus intently on you so will largely ignore other dogs in its vicinity, but dangerous encounters could be sparked if your dog thinks that another dog is muscling in on your attention. What I mean by this is that if you throw a dummy or a ball and two dogs go after it, it could cause conflict.

Dogs are nosy and can't resist having a look at what those nearby might be doing. You will get much more attention from your dog in a quiet and private place.

All sorts of things can distract your dog from its training. If you live in the country and there are animals such as sheep or, worse, bullocks in the next field, try to find somewhere that offers less in the way of distraction.

The Irresistible

Years ago I had to do a demonstration for a large group of farmers who knew a bit about what they were watching. In the field next to the display ground a herd of bullocks ran excitedly up and down the boundary fence.

I had allowed just twenty minutes to complete the routine tasks I had chosen to demonstrate but was still trying to make headway an hour later. Both of my dogs had performed exactly the same tasks many times before but were totally put off by the antics of the demented bovines, which they mistook for their target.

I have yet to meet a dog that can reliably resist the blandishments of a mad March hare. In the country, during late February and March, hares will sit in the middle of a field and 'box' each other. When a dog approaches they will sit and seemingly invite it to come closer. When the dog gets close the hares move off with the acceleration of a good sports car.

Too much to resist! The dog takes off after them and all the calls in the world stand little chance of bringing it back once in full flight. The strange thing is that the dog must know that it has no chance of catching a hare.

But you stand a fair chance of stopping this before it happens because friend dog seldom notices the hares until they move. If you can call your dog back before the hares run you will avoid it getting caught up in a futile chase. As the dog might not stop for hedges and other obstacles – such as a main road – it is advisable to take evasive action.

Fear Objects

Sometimes fear in a dog has pretty obvious causes. The silent flight of a hot-air balloon, followed by a noisy burst of its burner and another silence can terrify even a 'bomb proof' dog and send it into a real panic. I don't imagine that city dwellers are often troubled by such things but it might well happen when you're away on holiday.

A brass band suddenly striking up can send a normally stable dog completely over the edge, as can something simple like an escaped plastic carrier bag flapping in the wind.

Observe your dog to see what sort of things might terrify it and avoid those triggers. Don't get impatient – your dog will not be able to rationalise such things, and it is only by rationalising that fear can be overcome. Repeatedly exposing your dog to the same terror object can lead to the fear becoming fixed in its mind.

Pica (Pronounced 'Peeka')

I have included this strange phenomenon just in case it happens to your dog. If it does, you might think that your dog's case is unique. It isn't, quite a few young dogs will have a tendency to do it.

Pica is a behavioural problem that involves taking plastic or stones into the mouth, holding and then swallowing them. A friend of mine had a dog that kept doing this until apparently it had a host of stones in its stomach. Behaviourists say that it can develop as attention-seeking.

The dog picks up a stone and encourages you to take it back. It refuses to let go and then swallows it – whether by accident or intention I do not know.

If your dog is in danger of injuring itself, then go and see your vet, who will probably advise the use of a muzzle for a period of time.

I used to know a most energetic Springer Spaniel who just loved to run and retrieve stones that were thrown for it; the only difference was that it tended to give them back so that the game could be repeated. But beware, this could be a very dangerous game to start.

Coprophagia

It is normal for bitches to eat the faeces of their puppies in order to keep the nesting area clean but sometimes adult dogs will do the same thing. As a result, they may suffer vomiting, diarrhoea or other illnesses.

Sometimes coprophagia is caused by a medical condition, sometimes by hunger, and sometimes it is done in order to attract attention. I am not qualified to comment on the possible medical reasons.

My dog Jack has just started to eat faeces he finds in the garden. Before I take him to see the vet I shall try to break him of the habit. Every time he goes to do this he will receive the command to 'leave it'. In addition, I shall hide food that he really likes near to the offending temptation so that he eats that instead. (I think that a small pile of choc drops placed ten feet this side of the mess might just win this culinary competition.)

If neither of these ploys works, then I shall sprinkle white pepper on the faeces and encourage Jack to find what he is looking for. The sneezing and discomfort will stop him.

Other Dogs

The one thing that you cannot legislate for is other dogs. I can't even point at a particular breed of dog and say this one is dangerous or that one is safe. However, do bear in mind my previous comments about dogs bred to fight and the kind of people who find it desirable to have one.

I do not believe there is such a thing as a dog that is born bad but there are plenty of really bad owners. Lack of training does not make a dog aggressive but mistreatment can.

A dogfight can be traumatic for the owner and very damaging to the dog. Sadly, dogs have no sense of fair play: weight and size do not come into consideration in a dog's mind. It is not uncommon for any other dogs present to join in – on the side of the strongest dog.

The loving, 'domesticated' dog reverts in a flash to a wild animal. Sometimes there are warning signals and sometimes not. It is hard to predict when it might happen.

Even the most thorough training can evaporate at such moments and no amount of commands will stop the fight. In fact, if you try to command your dog during a fight you will make the situation worse by putting it at a disadvantage.

I had the most friendly and lovable Yellow Labrador who relished a good fight and would go out looking for trouble. He was wonderful with children and adults but awful with other dogs.

The best advice I can offer is to try to anticipate likely trouble and avoid it.

The advantage you have is that the training process should have brought about a much better understanding of your dog, including the ability to read its body language.

Also, because your training has been thorough you should be able to stop a fight before the event (but probably not during). I have noticed that the dogs I have trained are confident but not aggressive.

Your dog will sense trouble before you do and its body language will tell you that it has.

Rolling

Dogs *love* to roll in the most disgusting substances. Their aim seems to be to cover as much of themselves with it as they can. The smellier it is, the greater their delight.

Nothing I have read has suggested a reason for this strange behaviour. My unproven theory is that they do it to disguise their own body smell. The dog comes from a long line of predators that wear down their prey by persistence. If the hunters can disguise their own scent perhaps they can cause a degree of confusion in the prey animal. What I mean is that if a pack of wolves smells like the animal they are hunting, it aids the hunt. Maybe it allows the wolves to get closer to their quarry before it is alarmed.

I try my best to stop my dogs rolling, even though it is natural for them to do so. Apart from the unacceptable smell, there is also the risk of them picking up an infestation of fox mite, which does a dog's health no favours.

It is not difficult to tell a dog to 'leave it' once they are trained, but you will need eyes in the back of your head to be successful every time. Anyone who has bathed a dog in the solution designed to clear up fox mite, while wearing protective clothing and looking and feeling like a spaceman, would not want to do it twice.

Foxes inhabit towns as well as rural areas, so this warning applies to all dog owners.

Eating Sheep and Rabbit Droppings

I think the reason that dogs do this is probably similar to their penchant for rolling, except in this case there is possibly a nutritional or roughage benefit as well. My dogs steal Sheep Rolls straight from the bag when I go to feed the sheep in winter. The rolls have a grass-like texture and are similar to the droppings of grass-eating animals. My dogs were all brought up on farms and have always made a beeline for what both sheep and rabbits have processed through their bodies. I have not seen any ill-effects from their eating of such.

Postscript

For six years I worked for nothing as a non-stipendiary priest on the border between Shropshire and Staffordshire. It was a 'thank you' to my maker for putting a lost sheepdog in my path all those years ago. Now I have returned to my Celtic roots. It means a special and peaceful time for us and much quality time for our dogs.

My wife and I, plus our fifteen dogs, a small flock of sheep and our retired ducks, live on the rising ground of a valley in Wales above a winding river on which the sun glints invitingly. We are miles away from anywhere busy. It is quiet, with no traffic and very few passers-by.

At night it is as dark as a magician's cloak and the stars can be seen twinkling clearly in the heavens. Our days are spent with our dogs. We take as long as we like, no need to rush.

It is nearly sunset: in Devon it would be called 'dimsey' or 'dimity', the half-light that shows all things in a gentle, restrained, smudgy palette as though some subtle landscapist, at the height of his powers, had painted his finest.

My sheep munch their way steadily through the thick lush grass in the orchard. For once the grass is not greener on the other side. Their breath sends out small patches of mist and the quiet of the evening allows me to hear the tearing of each grassy mouthful.

I am sitting on an outcrop of rocks, seemingly unsupported, suspended high above a steep green valley that falls away sharply in front of me.

At its lowest point a bluey mist sends advance tendrils slowly over the tussocks of grass like a soft tide exploring the line of least resistance.

The March pasture is lustrous green, and becoming damp and cool as evening takes over from day.

At first the impression is one of silence, but on closer listening, birds are gently singing the last notes of the day. Rabbits and foxes will be thinking of venturing out.

I bring a different group of dogs here each evening, in a sort of fairness rota. This time it is Muppet, Misty, Susie and Bendi. They know that this walk is different from their dashing-all-over-the-place daytime walks.

We sit together, like eagles in their eyrie, surveying the tranquil pasture below us. They lean in so that their bodies touch my legs. Muppet, Misty and Bendi (the dog in the iron mask) cuddle closer while Susie, restless, ever moving, ceaselessly exploring, looks in each fern or bramble patch for some great excitement.

On the way back we will pass an old cast-iron cattle trough filled with cool spring water. Three of the dogs will stand on their back legs and slurp the wonderful water. Misty, of the damaged hip, will stand and look at me meaningfully. She wants me to take the water in cupped hands and offer it at a more reachable height.

Of course I do so, as she knew I would. She drinks from my hands, her cool tongue brushing my palms.

Peace is dog-shaped. Contentment wears a black-and-white furry suit.

Index

Note: All references are to dogs unless otherwise indicated.

tone of voice (humans) 68, 111,
    208, 262
toys 213–14
training
    see also commands
    adjustment for different dogs
        260–61
    assessment of dogs 257–60
    balls 96–7
    bridge between close and
        distance work 71–9
    'come back' command 29, 85,
        93–101
    for different breeds 165–8
    distractions 265
    dummies 166
    each dog separately 120, 261–3
    gentle approach 159–60
    keeping dog close 68–9
    languages 188, 261–2
    layers of command 78–9
    leads 29, 55–9, 224–5
    learning from older dogs 149
    'lie down' command 29, 65, 68
    maintaining 170
    moment of fruition 247–53
    older dogs 191
    partnership between trainer and
        dog 60–61
    quiet environment 265
    right and left 167
    routines 197–8
    single trainer 69
    'sit' command 29, 65, 66–7
    'stand' command 29, 65, 70

'stop' command 29, 58, 59, 98,
    99
toilet training 47–52
treats 59, 96
'walk slowly' command 76–7
whistled commands 85, 98–9
treats 59, 96
trust, bond of with puppy 44–5

Ueno, Eisaburo 242
understanding, lack of (owners)
    5–6, 21, 138–9

vets 227–35
    qualities 234–5
    right knowledge 232–4
visitors, dogs' reaction to 203–5
voice, tone of (humans) 68, 111,
    208, 262

'walk on' command 29, 58
'walk slowly' command 76–7
weaning 42, 147
    see also mother dogs, removal of
        puppies from
welcoming gestures 96–7
Whippets 168
whistled commands 81–5, 98–9
whistles 81–5
wild dogs 129
Wing (dog) 4, 39
Wire-haired Terriers 41
wolves 123, 124–5, 129, 135–6, 139
wrestling with dogs (play) 134